EARLY in 1952, Stephen Spender travelled from Marseilles to Haifa on a "children's boat", escorting boys and girls from Europe and North Africa to new homes in Israel. *Learning Laughter*, which he calls "a travel book with a theme", is his story of how, in the midst of its many problems, Israel is working to rehabilitate its youngest generation.

The author toured the settlements in Israel where children from more than thirty countries are living together. Some of the settlements were founded by Youth Aliyah, an organisation which for twenty years has rescued children from persecution. Many of the boys and girls Mr. Spender met had lost parents and other relatives during the war. Many had themselves suffered incredible cruelties. Yet, united to build together a national home, they were learning to forget the past, learning to laugh again.

Mr. Spender took a good look at the new country as a whole, account of his journey ery enlightening reading. critical observer, and does re the tremendous ob- which confront Israel in eriments in communal and new educational He notes the diffi- which face adults, who new way of life harder their children. His ces in Israel are told with d of disarming sincerity wd insight which makes of the best descriptive n the current scene.

Laughter is imaginatively d with photographs, hem taken by the author.

EN SPENDER was born in 1909, near London. He attended Oxford and published his first book, *Twenty Poems*, in 1930. The publication of *Poems* (1933) brought him fame as one of the leading poets of the generation. He has published several books of prose and poetry since then, including another travel book, *European Witness* (1945), and his autobiography, *World Within World* (1951).

LEARNING LAUGHTER

Learning
LAUGHTER

BY
STEPHEN SPENDER

HARCOURT, BRACE AND COMPANY, INC
NEW YORK

To Vera Weizmann.

CONTENTS

LIST OF ILLUSTRATIONS

Photographs 1 to 6 by RIWKIN of Stockholm

INTRODUCTION

THIS book is based on the journal of a tour in Israel made in the spring of 1952. Impressions are grouped around a study of Youth Aliyah, the organization which has cared for 60,000 children brought from all parts of the world to Israel.

The organizers of Youth Aliyah asked me to write about their work. I accepted their invitation thinking that I would write a travel book and not just the story of an organization; and this I have stuck to.

The idea of a travel book with a theme appeals to me. Impressions inevitably superficial should, I think, acquire proportion and direction, if they are related to a central subject.

Moreover, Youth Aliyah quite naturally took me beyond the problems of the children to those of Israel; and those of Israel brought me back to the children.

In the lives of these children, brought from every part of the world where there are Jews, and in those of other young Israelis a nation will be born. If the conception of an Israeli not just as Palestinian "sabra," nor as Western nor Oriental Jew, but as a citizen who embraces within his being the whole world from which the Jews have come into Israel—if such a world-conscious yet home-returned Jew is not born in this generation of the Ingathered children, then—as these pages may show—the 20th Century Jewish nation may fall apart into Western and Eastern, white and coloured Jews who happen to live together—and who will violently disagree—in Israel.

To study the children is to study the germ of the New State. It is also, incidentally, the most charming and delightful introduction to a nation already beset with many problems.

At the same time, it would be unreal to look at the children without looking also at Israel itself: for just as Israel's future is in the lives of the children, so the children are bound up with the present state of their country. If things go from bad to worse with Israel, the children will have less chance of fulfilling the tasks which have been thrust—perhaps too eagerly—upon them. If things go well, the promise of the children has the greater chance of being fulfilled.

The children led me to Israel, and Israel led me back to the children. That is the circular movement which is, I hope, reflected in the form of this book, the stages of this little journey.

But the problems of Israel also lead at every turn to wider problems.

It often struck me, while I was there, that several things the Jews were doing which seemed perhaps far too uncommon sense in their circumstance, would make very good sense indeed in other parts of the world.

For example, immigration is partly the result of the terrible needs of world Jewry, partly a demonstration of Zionist principle carried out almost regardless of other considerations. In Israel it exposes the country to tremendous risks and introduces more people into what are already relatively crowded areas.

But if Christians—for instance—had the sense of being a world community, what problems might be solved by the willingness of populations to be shifted for reasons other than short-term self-interest. With a little of the zeal of Israel, people could be shifted out of crowded areas into empty ones, and parts of the world now exposed to attack because they are depopulated could be made to weigh against their more crowded neighbours. Religion (for I believe that the impulse of Zionism is basically religious) enables the Jews to carry out a world-migration even against common sense. If ethical feeling could be combined with common sense in other parts of the world,

Israel shows that it might be possible to make willingly those shifts in population which would solve many problems.

So also with the children. The Israelis are confronted with the immense problem of getting people ingathered from 30 different nations, and having nothing in common but that they are Jews, to live together. The harmonious concept "Jew" must be made to drive out the barriers of origin and colour which threaten the unity of Israel. The significance of Youth Aliyah is that it is a movement to create this harmony among the children.

So also might we teach our children, by the practice of living together, that they have a common humanity which ignores barriers.

Not that I think Youth Aliyah perfect. As the reader will see I approach it with an open mind, and often in a critical spirit. As in the whole Israeli educational system, the great good which is being done in teaching the children to regard themselves as members of a single Jewish community, is to some extent undone by dividing them into groups whose education is directed by different political parties—and there is Jewish nationalism as well.

All the same, the politicizing of education is quite unnecessary. It is the disease of the parents which the children need never acquire were they not taught it. The lesson of Youth Aliyah that children can be brought up without sharing the mutual hostility of their parents—based on colour of skin and place of origin—remains true.

I have to thank all those in Israel whom I interviewed and who are mentioned in these pages—particularly those who were my companions on so many journeys. I have also to thank Mr. Sholom J. Kahn for generously allowing me to quote from his translation of the lines of Uri Zvi Greenberg; Mr. Ramati who took me in the Negev; and Mr. Michaelis who supplied me with notes about this trip. I wish also to thank the organizers

of the British Youth Aliyah committee—particularly Lady
Low, Mrs. Miriam Warburg and Mr. Otto Zarek and also the
Consul of Israel in London, Mr. P. Leshem.

CHAPTER I

THE ARTZA ETCETERA

MY first glimpse of the children was from the car of Mr.
Lutz, as we turned the corner of the drive leading up to
the large villa, the *Maison de Transit*, on the outskirts of
Marseilles. It was a tall stucco pinkish-yellowing house, and
the children were peeping through the shrubs of its rocky
hillside garden. Between branches leering masks peered and
emitted yells or whoops. Then we went up to a terrace in front
of the house overlooking the blue bay, and there were many
more children, also wearing masks, singing and dancing. All
but three, that is to say, who were sobbing out a dirge-like
unmelodious wail, and screening their faces in their hands
from the others, as though they felt shut out from the rest of
the group.

These three must be left behind, Mr. Lutz explained, because
they suffered from the "trachome volant", contagious trachoma.
The other children had been cured of the various diseases they
brought with them from Morocco, of which trachoma is the
most prevalent.

We went into the house and had breakfast in a bare room.
It consisted of large hunks of brownish bread, dollops of
butter and sweetish tea poured out of a jug into cups without
handles. Seated with us were two girls of the rather thick and
sportive type, who looked after the children, and the sensitive,
dreamy looking brothers whose names, I learned, were Feigenbaum, Jews from Poland on their way to Israel. Isvi was dark,
the other—whose name I didn't get—sandy-haired. Both had

5

the keen, sensitive, intelligent expression on oval quick-eyed faces which I have seen often on the faces of French students: I found myself searching for any specifically Jewish quality in these brothers, and thought perhaps it lay in a kind of soft sadness which blurred their brightest smiles, the aura, the halo of suffering which is often like a charm on the young Jew. They carried farewellingly on throughout breakfast with the two girls.

In all the Transit House there seemed hardly any furniture. The decorations consisted of one or two children's drawings, and artistically pretentious posters dramatizing the potentialities and the needs of Israel. After breakfast I went down to the old port at Marseilles and I felt that I already belonged to the world of handleless mugs and the austere breakfast, and it would be wrong to sit at one of the little restaurants set round the small harbour like paintings round the walls of a gallery, with their images of prawns, red mullets, sea urchins, oysters and some other shell-fish that looked like an old and succulent root, pressing against my senses.

Anyway I had money for nothing except to collect together envelopes, typing and carbon paper, and notebooks, none of which—Mr. Lutz had told me—was easily obtainable in Israel. Having a weakness for writing materials, I spent 3,000 francs on these things. Now I had only 2,000 francs remaining to spend on board ship during six days—just enough for tips, if I was lucky, and nothing over for drinks.

I returned to the Transit Centre for luncheon cooked by Madame Lutz and served in the private quarters of her husband and herself, with a simplicity reminding me of the Quakers (of whom I was often to think later in Israel). On our way to this room, we passed the large dining room where the immigrant children, seated at long tables were finishing their last meal at the Transit Centre. As we came in they started to sing hymns which took the form of a chorus composed of "the rest" answering a soloist. The boys wore tweed caps the peaks of which, above their widely separated brown eyes and bronzed features, gave them a wooden, puppet-like appearance.

After the meal we came downstairs again to a ground-floor room where the children, dressed and labelled for the journey, were lined up in two rows. They were given a pep-talk by Mr. Lutz. He told them not to lose their tickets, and exhorted each to be an example to the others. Especially, when they got down to the quay-side they should not hand their papers to any stranger purporting to represent the steamship company. When they got to Israel—Mr. Lutz continued—they would no longer be Moroccans or exiles, they would be little Israelis. If they broke a window it would be *their window* they were breaking, if they trampled on a tree, their tree. Mr. Lutz hoped they wouldn't be called on to do what so many of their brothers had done—give their lives for the new country. But if they were not asked to die, then they should be all the more proud to *live* for Israel.

The children listened with an air of solemn attentiveness. Then they passed out on to the terrace where their austere suit-cases—many of which the owners had painted with garish-coloured stripes—were set down on the path. On this baggage of a cheap, mass-produced dullness, the children had scrawled their bright signatures of the bazaar. Conversely, their town suits and caps were the imprints of Western uniformity set on them. The struggle between the garish stripes on the suit-cases and the town-caps on the heads, was something I was to see a good deal of. Now buses arrived and the children were packed into them—all except the wailing trio whom we left gazing down at the sea over the cliff-like edge of the villa terrace.

A couple of hours later, as I stood on board the *Artza*, I saw the children wait in a "crocodile" on the quay, becapped still, suit-cases in hand, identification labels on jacket lapels, and apparently not having lost their tickets, for they all got on board.

The *Artza* was packed with people of all nations: from

America, France, Russia, Germany, Poland, Roumania, Egypt, Persia, Iraq, Morocco—just to name a few. It was still more packed with their belongings, for everyone seemed, like me, to have heard that there was nothing whatever to be obtained in Israel. Parcels containing food-stuffs, radio-sets and other belongings, flowed out of cabins into corridors and were even jammed into such spaces as that between the wash-basin and the floor of the W.C. My cabin—which I had hoped I was going to have alone in order to study during the voyage—was filled with an immigrant from Poland, and with sacks of onions he had brought with him. Various other parcels heaping up the cabin put an end to my hopes of work by making the writing table inaccessible.

At the captain's table, my fellow guests were the engineer Albert Margolis and his wife. Margolis, with his pince-nez, his intelligently philosophic, faintly cynical, considering air, reminded me of one of those detached characters (himself capable of passionate feeling) in Turgenev or Chehov, who sums up the lives of other people. He was travelling to Israel for the purpose of constructing a machine for sorting out different kinds of citreous fruit.

He was a man with independent views, and a personal philosophy. His attitude to the country to which he was going was one of sympathy for its aims only equalled by his detachment about the methods used by Israelis. His statuesque, beautifully dressed wife must have had an extremely unpleasant voyage. Owing to an illness which was the result of the Moroccan climate, she could eat almost nothing of the fare provided by the *Artza*.

The captain was a cordial, smilingly rotund man in early middle life. For some reason I guessed almost as soon as I saw him that he came from Hamburg. He gave me the feeling of the genial smiling individualism of that city. Jews often make one think more instantly of their place of origin than do the natives of that place.

One day—rather remarkably for the Mediterranean—we saw whales playing not very far from the bows of the ship. They looked like immense dolphins as they skidded out of the sea revealing keel-like bellies, and lashing tails, with lines cold and clear-curling as an engraving. I could hardly believe they were really whales, but at dinner that night the captain confirmed that it was so. Margolis remarked that some whales lived off microscopic organisms contained in sea-water. "That is a mystery of feeding that we haven't learned how to make use of," he said with his slightly mysterious smile. "For instance if you shape a cloth like a net and drag it from the stern of a boat, after a few hours the interior will be covered with a green-ish slime. This slime is nutritive and if we knew how to exploit it, people who find themselves shipwrecked on rafts without food would not have to die of starvation."

A thought perhaps suggested by going to Israel, I afterwards reflected . . .

During the first three days the voyage was pleasanter than I had expected. I had dramatized the *Artza* as a kind of hell-ship packed with people singing Hebrew melodies and without material comforts. Actually the food was good, and it was only its being about twice as crowded as most ships, and that we had indifferent weather, which made the voyage rather unnerving.

Twenty-four hours after leaving Marseilles we passed Corsica; a coastline of rocky mountains the colour and texture of sandpaper—blobs of trees above and shadows below—against an oily sky smeared with a few clouds. Below the ruled line at the base of this coast, and beyond the undulating belt of the sea, shone a long yellow strip of beach.

A day later the passengers crowded on deck to see Stromboli rise isosceles out of the waves. One white and one grey cloud were stuck into the top of the volcanic island like feathers in a hat. On one side a chute of lava formed a single sliding wall. From the ship we saw houses on a green shelf above a rock-cliff.

This was a day of sights. For the same evening we passed

through the Straits of Messina, partly hidden by the darkness beneath clouds like billowing sails white-bellying above the mountain tops. The coastline of the toe of Italy looked as if a rake had been dragged along it leaving parallel lines of undulating strata in the rock. The *Artza* moved under the gaze of Palermo across the waters at Messina, Messina at Palermo. The waves around us seemed on a leash dragged back by the currents, snapping and foaming at the jaws like dogs. As we moved on, darkness fell and Messina, sparkling with scattered lights, seemed lost in grey slate under the densely black heights of the mountains weighed on by tons of even blacker clouds.

The Moroccan children and the other many-nationed third-class passengers, crowded forward on to the bows of the ship as we passed through the Straits. To do this they had to work their way past two buses, many other bulky objects, and washing hung on lines, which cumbered the third-class deck. Most of these passengers looked more Arab than Jew. Some of them were old, and a few looked sick or demented.

The children slept in a large dormitory in the exact centre of the ship. It had no daylight, but in other ways seemed comfortable, as, although crowded, there was space between the rows of bunks.

During these first few days I had some conversations with Isvi Feigenbaum, who told me he was a Youth Aliyah educator in a Kibbutz. The children on the ship—he explained—were "religious" children from an orthodox community in Morocco. This, indeed, they demonstrated by going on to the upper deck and singing their clanging hymns from time to time. Isvi said that in Casablanca, Oran, Tangiers and the other places these children came from, they live in a grinding poverty, often in caves or in small rooms containing 14 or 15 inhabitants. They go out to work at the age of eight, and in the towns they are usually corrupted by the time they reach adolescence. Very few of them come from good homes. All arrive at the French training centres at Montpellier and near Marseilles, equipped with

1. Off to school

2. Citizens of one country

3. Oriental children learning Hebrew

4. A Youth Aliyah boy
helps his little brother

knives, distrustful, suspicious and suffering from various diseases.

Within three months, the transformation (which was certainly noticeable among the children on the *Artza*) has begun. The children have learned the three basic essentials of their training: politeness, cleanliness and a certain ability to co-operate with one another and with the teachers.

Isvi told me that when they arrive in Israel they feel a sense of inferiority towards the children from European countries. But they also enjoy certain advantages. They are used to a very hard life and conditions in Israel, although hard, are superior to those they have known in the places they come from.

He said that some of the Moroccan children learned quickly and easily and were glad to do so. Others fell into a rage at the idea that they should have to know anything. Some of them became violent and on one occasion he had been attacked with a knife by a boy who resented being taught the alphabet.

On the third day of the voyage the ship started rolling and it continued to do so all the way to Haifa.

The voyage now changed—as voyages, I find, often do—from a sea cure into a minor illness which could only be cured by arriving on land. I spent most of my time on my bunk, trying to ignore the sweetish smell of the onions in the cabin, mingling with all the other smells in the ship, not the least sickly of which to my nostrils was now the Jewish way of cooking. In rapid succession I read *Henry V*, *The Tempest*, *King Lear*, and *Cymbeline*. Then I followed these with the posthumously published notebook of André Gide—*Les Jeux sont Faits*—*Mrs. Dalloway*—which was in the ship's library—and the *Fleurs du Mal* I had bought in Marseilles. I translated the first stanza of a poem of Baudelaire, and then got stuck:

> Mother of memories, mistress of mistresses,
> Thou all my joy, my task of delight,
> Recall now the beauty of our caresses,

B

> The calm of the hearth and the charm of the night,
> Mother of memories, mistress of mistresses.

Such study in a gap between home and a job of work is valuable, I think. It is an enforced period of retreat and reflection.

I had the illusion that I understood Shakespeare as I had never done before: not only intellectually (and I made a great effort to follow every line) but also with muscles of my inmost being. With the ship rolling, I developed theories about Shakespeare's later manner: that it is a kind of shorthand in which thought is packed thickly into cases which have a supreme simplicity. Each speech by each character has a direction like a pointing arrow and that this arrow passes through a dozen other meanings does not matter. So Shakespeare is not, even in the last plays, an obscure writer: he is a writer whose elemental simplicities contain many complex obscurities, and whose directions include as well as overcome difficulties.

Can he, though—I asked myself—be said to write well in *A Winter's Tale* and *Cymbeline?* The answer is that for his purposes—which care for none outside these particular plays—the manner is extremely effective. But it is unprecedented and to imitate it is to court catastrophe. Yet "writing well" surely means driving a public vehicle of expressive language in which others can ride and which others can drive. That is what the 18th Century achieved in the unbarbarous style of their prose and their heroic couplets; and they judged Shakespeare not to have done just this. A barbarous style is a wild chariot a genius whips along by himself.

Queasy thoughts in a cabin which managed to remain stuffy even when door and port-hole were wide open and a gale howling through. I had managed to persuade my cabin-mate to park the onions elsewhere; but their odour remained.

From the cabin, I went to the main saloon and bar—permanently crowded with parents and their children, who were becoming more uninhibited with every knot we went, and

more difficult for their imploring, threatening parents to cope
with. Isvi, his brother, a sensitive-looking French Jewish boy
and two girls sat at a table playing cards. Shutting out the din,
serious-looking pairs from Riga and Roumania, Germany and
Egypt, sat playing endless games of chess, surrounded by
appraising connoisseurs. Two young Americans visiting Israel
walked around, glamorously free of the pasts and futures
surrounding them. A hefty young farmer from a Kibbutz sat
alone in a corner reading the Marx-Engels correspondence.
Behind the bar, the barman with handlebar moustaches tried
to adjust the radio-gramophone so that it could play someone's
records of Beethoven's Seventh which he was taking back to
his Kibbutz. The ship rolled too much and the needle jumped
the grooves—an effect itself likely to add to the general feeling
of nausea and discomfort. Margolis with his sceptical smile and
faintly raised nostrils moved benevolently from group to group,
carrying on conversations in half a dozen languages.

The Moroccan children were being sick in their dormitory
amidships. Fewer and fewer managed to stagger on deck and
grind out a religious song. Their faces began to look like badly
varnished wood going green and yellow at the edges. One day,
the captain invited the Margolises and me to tea in his cabin.
He told us that his crew was composed of as many nationals as
the United Nations—and not all of them Jews. The *Artza* was a
ship of German origin. It had been "mother" ship to U-boats
during the war, succouring them with fuel in mid-Atlantic.
Then it had become one of those crowded, overladen ships
which took illegal immigrants to Palestine after the war, during
the period of the Mandatory Government.

So the *Artza* had after all been through seas of blood and
crime, and my reason for going on this voyage was to share this
with her and with the children who were being borne to the
land of their rebirth, like the unborn spirits in Maeterlinck's
play the "Blue Bird."

This remained true even though the rather dull experience

did not correspond at all to my fantasy voyage which had been more vivid than this week's nausea. But it provided a space in which I could become aware of my reason for accepting Youth Aliyah's invitation to Israel.

For many months before this journey, I have had an idea at the back of my mind which is so obvious that I myself know hardly what to think of it; and yet it goes on haunting me.

It is simply this; that the main divisions which we are told exist in the contemporary world—divisions between capitalists and proletarians, East and West, nation and nation—would become unnecessary if we could get one idea firmly enough into the minds of the adults: that the true division of the world is not these, but that between adults and children.

Of course, the other divisions are very real to adults. They are indeed so firmly fixed in the lives of every grown up person that—as between people over a certain age—it is impossible to get rid of them among contemporaries.

All the same, when things have got to a certain point—when for example, a whole generation is faced with the fact that their rivalries may lead to the destruction of all existing civilization— then it seems reasonable to reflect that these interests, these rivalries, these hatreds and fears which are a machinery working in them more potently than their minds and hearts — after all don't exist at all in the lives of the children.

And it should be possible to go on from this thought to one that follows on it: that the world in fact is the children, and that if we say the world will be destroyed we mean nothing else but that the children will be destroyed; for we adults are on our way out already.

However enormous and compulsive our claims, they are all shadowy, except in so far as they exist within the lives of our children. If our children are not going to have lives, then these claims are a shadow that casts no shadow. They cease to be realities.

The aristocrat when he defends his place in society is defend-

ing his heirs; the worker when he fights for his rights, is fighting
for a future in which his children will be able to enjoy advantages which he has not had. The nations when they seek power
over one another, are seeking for a world in which the children
of one nation will rule over those of another.

But if all these claims become cancelled out in total destruction, then it is possible to look at the world and to see no other
division except that between the young and the old.

And to-day the old have become totally prey to their unreal
claims. The adult world is a place in which the worker cannot
give way to the capitalist, nor the capitalist to the worker, nor
the rulers of one nation to those of another nation, nor the
East to the West nor the West to the East. Something much
more than loss of material interests is concerned; and this is
loss of prestige. For loss of prestige in a world of tensions such
as ours means a promissory note by the loser to the gainer that
he will gain still more. And this is of course intolerable, because
it means that the loser must either stop losing at some time or
lose everything.

The adults have got into a situation where they cannot
resolve their own problems in their relations with one another.
They ought to admit to a universal bankruptcy in all the coinage
of international and inter-class intercourse, which makes
negotiation impossible. If they admitted to such a bankruptcy,
they then might accept a kind of stand-still arrangement, in
which they concentrated their attention on the one interest
that all have in common: their children.

It is difficult to think that even in the present state of the
world people would admit openly that they wanted to murder
each other's children: still less that they wished to murder all
the children all over the world.

But if they consider the fate of the children then they must
admit that these famous interests which so dominate the lives
of the parents are no fatality, no compulsion, no Greek doom
in the minds of the children at all; except of course in so far as

they have reached an age to have destructive ideas put into their heads by the adults.

A capitalist child does not even know what it is to be a capitalist, nor a proletarian a proletarian. Left alone in the same street the little capitalists play with the little proletarians without knowing that they are doing any wrong. And so with the children of coloured and white peoples, of Easterners and Westerners.

The interests of the adults are only projected into the lives of their children in so far as the adults believe that the children are going to benefit. The rich want their children to inherit, in order that they may be happier than if they were poor, the workers want their children to enjoy the fruits of revolution, and so on.

But if, as I have said, all these interests can no longer be projected into the lives of the children, because the conflict between the adults has reached a stage when it can achieve nothing except the destruction of the future of most of the human race, then the adults are no longer fighting *for* but only against the children. The problem then is to teach the children to adapt themselves to a situation which is obvious to all, in which they cannot inherit the interests and attitudes of their parents. This of course, is difficult, not because the children are innately nationalist or class conscious, but because it would be difficult for the parents to stop influencing the children to adopt their attitudes.

Still, given a complete realization of the situation, it could be done. What is required is that the adults should admit openly the dilemma they are in: that they cannot, amongst themselves, abandon their interests or their need for prestige. Admitting this, though, they must also admit that if they pursue their aims their children will be destroyed. They must agree then to concentrate on the problem of saving the children. The whole adult world must think about the children and how to resolve the problems which divide the world of to-day within the lives of the children to-morrow.

Now the State of Israel, in its small way, is confronted with just such a problem of rivalries amongst groups of adults which it is endeavouring to solve in the lives of the children. The attempt is incomplete; for the educators are concerned with making a new nation, and teaching the children to hate their national enemies; and in addition to this they are instilling ideological passions into their minds. All the same, the Israelis, in order to create a nation, have to deal with children coming from many nations, and therefore the training they give to children often of different colour, in living together, is an experiment in internationalism. It is an attempt to raise the children out of the situation in which Western Jews are suspicious of the Orientals, and to teach all these children to belong to one nation. The Jews, coming from all the different nations of the world, are the whole world within a small compass; and that which to them is being Jews would be for the rest of us, if we educated the children to think of one another as the same—regardless of colour, race or place of birth—humanity.

CHAPTER II

HAIFA

O^N March 18th, after six days on the Mediterranean we arrived at Haifa at dawn. When I went on deck it was beginning to grow light. The ship had hoisted a flag which signified that the health authorities should come on board. The grey dawn lightened and then became filled with colour and we saw the curved bay of Haifa, with its monastery-surmounted hills around us, and the little improvised jetties stretching out into the sea. The Feigenbaum brothers, the tough young farmer from the Kibbutz who read Karl Marx, and the sensitive French Jew, stood on deck making quite silly remarks. There was a feeling of tears under their delighted laughter. They counted every ship they saw, as though upon their fingers. Seeing a tugboat one of them shouted: "That's our navy." Seeing an aeroplane fly overhead: "And that's our air force." But suddenly, with a sweeping gesture of his arm, which indicated the whole coastline, Isvi exclaimed to the French boy in a quite different tone of voice: "Regarde, c'est tout à nous." It was as though they had fallen to their knees with tears of gratitude.

Significantly enough he was corrected at once by another of their group, who remarked soberly that *au contraire* the Northernmost point of the bay that they could see was already Lebanon. "It's such a little country, ours." Yet this sense of the littleness of Israel, joined hands with what had previously been said.

After what seemed an endless wait, I was allowed off the

ship, and met by Mr. Melitz, representative of Youth Aliyah, appointed to show me round during my first few days in Israel. Grey-haired, sunburned, wearing an open-necked shirt and flannel trousers, reminding me of a distinguished-looking school teacher, he immediately started explaining things. Formerly the port of Haifa was run by Arab labour, but when the Israeli State was declared, the Arabs all assembled at the quayside and insisted on leaving, although it was explained to them that if they stayed, they would come to no harm.

Fortunately, anticipating this situation, Jews in Haifa had trained themselves to take over the administration of the port (which now functions very well, said Mr. Melitz), although one of the arguments of the Mandatory Government had been that the Jews would be incapable of running the port. But the oil refineries are not functioning because the Arabs have cut the oil pipe-line.

We drove to the hotel above the main part of the town, where I stayed. It was in the modern German style, and in green and cool surroundings.

In the afternoon, he fetched me from the hotel and we went to the large Youth Aliyah sorting out centre near Haifa. This was formerly a British military camp. It consists of huts spread out on the hillside looking out through beautiful trees, over the sea. The landscape of the encampment had been developed by the groups of Youth Aliyah children passing through.

The round-faced, hearty-mannered director took me into the office and told me about the children in his care. Children arrive from every part of the world at the rate of about 350 in three to four weeks. They are medically examined, and their futures are decided on here. They go from the sorting out centre to as many as 200 different places. The main groupings of the children are: from North Africa, 2,000; from Iraq, 1,500; from Roumania, 1,000; from Persia, 600.

I asked how long the children wait at the Centre, and he said on the average from two to three weeks, though sometimes, for reasons of physical or psychological health, for a much longer time.

He outlined to me the system of house-mothers and educators, and of leaders chosen from among themselves, who care for the children. The children arrive in groups, like the one I had accompanied on the *Artza*, or with their parents.

In the early days before there was any problem of the Oriental Jews, and Youth Aliyah was composed—as we shall see—of children rescued from Hitler, the organization was designed to deal with children who had been separated for many years—and perhaps for always—from their parents. But since— even in the early days—the parents for the most part were not dead, but only separated from their children, the attitudes of the absentee parents towards the educators and of the educators towards them, became very controversial.

In the early days, when Youth Aliyah was simply an organization for getting Jewish children out of the hands of Hitler, the separation from their children was something which those parents who remained in Germany and Europe, had agreed to, however reluctantly.

But with the new immigration of the so-called "Oriental" children from Africa and Asia, the parents sometimes accompany the children to Israel. They nearly always follow them there eventually. In either case they may wish to have the children back to live with them—perhaps because they intended to send the children temporarily to institutions while they themselves were settling down in their new home; or perhaps because, arriving in Israel themselves, they wish the family to be reunited.

The reader may think that the parents should certainly have their own children. And in fact, they do often claim and get them. But in many cases there are good reasons why the educators should wish to get the children away from the "eastern" parents.

For one thing, the conditions in which the parents—through

no fault of their own—have to live during the first two years
after their arrival, are those of the miserable slum-like encampments called the ma'abara. But the main reason is that the
Westernized Jews who developed the Jewish State on the soil
of Palestine long before it was actually founded, regard the
family life of the Eastern Jew with horror.

It is all very well, they say, being sentimental about the
family. But the Eastern family means the complete domination
of the children by a tyrannic father. The boys are sent out to
work at the age of 10 or 11: and in conditions as they are to-day
this means that they are sent on to the Black Market. The girls
are imprisoned within a slavish ignorance, and kept in slavish
conditions.

Moreover—and here one encounters the ambivalence which
is found so often in Israel—we need to change the attitudes
of the orientals, and we can only do so by getting hold of the
children. We have brought them into Israel—or encouraged
them to come—but we do not want the country orientalized.
If we let the children remain with their parents, they will
grow up to establish the conditions of the Mellah and the Black
Market. If we take them away, we may teach them to become
good Israeli citizens.

In this way we shall be able to accomplish a change in a few
years which otherwise might not be made for generations.
Indeed, if we don't make this change, there is a danger of the
increasingly Oriental population—which is likely soon to
become the majority—changing the country to adopt their
ways.

As they sometimes put it: "Moses had to take the Children of
Israel into the desert for 40 years in order to change them;
but we hope to accomplish the same transformation in the
Promised Land, in a far shorter time. We can only do this,
though, if we have the children."

This touches on a theme which I shall be brought back to
many times in these pages: the relationship of the Western with

the Oriental Jews. Meanwhile though, I asked the director how
the Eastern children got it into their heads to come to Israel.
He replied that in Morocco and Tunisia representatives of the
Zionist organization do propaganda for the Ingathering of the
Jews into the New State. The idea of returning to Jerusalem
and the Promised Land is central to the Jewish faith, particularly in the Eastern countries. The response of the Jews has
been overwhelming, especially among the poorer classes. No
representatives of the Israeli immigration authorities have been
allowed into Roumania and Iraq. Yet, as the figures I have
quoted above show, the response in those countries has nonetheless been very great.

I witnessed the arrival of the Moroccan children whom I
had left on board ship. Each was given a piece of soap, a towel,
a few clothes and a little coil of raffia to serve as combined
sponge and scrubbing brush. They seemed already, in their
few hours ashore, to have entered into the new life of the camp,
and they greeted me as an old friend from a forgotten past.
They were smiling excitedly and their eyes shone through the
shadow of the corrugated iron shed where they collected these
belongings.

We went out into the bright sunlight of a broad path between
lines of huts. Each hut had a little garden constructed rather
crudely around it, planted with gaudy flowers. The director
told me that as soon as the children arrived at the Sorting Out
Centre, they are set to do household tasks and cultivate the
garden. It is important that they should be plunged directly
into a stream of activities.

In some gardens, past generations of immigrant children had
made miniature buildings—houses built of pebbles, a fountain,
a mill. Some mosaics of plants and fish had been done by a boy
who was skilled in this work and who had stayed several weeks
at the camp. He had made a fountain with a mosaic of a goose
in the bowl, and also a sundial with the signs of the zodiac on

it: all in a style which went back more than 2,000 years.

We went into several of the huts. In one there was a collection of things made by the children—soft toys—dogs and cats and other animals—stitched belts, woollen rugs, bowls of papier maché on which you could read the lettering of newspaper through the transparent paint and varnish.

The interiors of the huts showed a certain imaginative effort which had gone into making the most of very limited possibilities. The girls were put into huts slightly more elegant— Swedish pre-fabs—than those of the boys. Three Moroccan girls, black-eyed, mischievous looking, lolled on their beds, laughing and rolling their eyes at us. With a few decorations and flowers and their own animal figures they managed to produce an effect reminiscent of a harem, painted by Delacroix.

The boys' huts were barer and plainer, but clean and airy. Attempts had been made to enliven them with decorations scratched on the walls. The mattresses of some of the beds were badly torn and stained.

In one of the dormitories there was a group of Roumanian boys. We talked with Reuben Butnera, a tall blue-eyed peasant child with a rather solemn, swollen expression, as though he might at any moment burst into tears. He told Melitz that since his arrival in Israel he had been with his parents in Beer-Sheba some five months, without learning to do anything. He said he would like now to learn a profession. "What do you want to be?" Melitz asked. "A locksmith or a carpenter," was the reply. "Ah," Melitz commented to me. "Nowadays they all answer in that way. They do not want to go on to the land. Agronomy is also a very nice profession," he insisted to the boy who murmured unenthusiastically and hung his head. We left him sitting on his bed staring in front of him through misty blue eyes.

Before going, however, I tried to find out what was the position of the Jews to-day in Roumania under the communist regime. I gathered that the Jews are being persecuted not so much for racial reasons as because they belong to a class of small merchants in process of liquidation. I reflected that this class is not wanted, either, in Israel, where boys like Reuben are talked out of being small traders and talked into being collective farmers. I wonder whether the Jews will be more successful in talking the Jews out of their commercial operations than the Gentiles have been.

We went out of the hut into the grounds again, where a dusky-skinned, black-haired, black-eyed gipsy looking boy stood sullenly staring at us. Mr. Melitz snatched the boy's peaked sun-cap off his head turned it inside out and jocularly put it back on his head again upside down. The boy smiled with what seemed only a minimal polite response as though to say "We are not amused." "How long have you been here?" · asked Mr. Melitz. "Six months," the boy answered. "Why six months?" The boy shrugged his shoulders and seemed unable to explain. Growing more friendly, he lifted up his jersey and revealed that his body was covered with scars from knife-wounds. He appeared to be one of the "difficult" children.

For tea we now went to a hut where a group of children were listening to a man playing the banjo. This man had something *louche* about his appearance which contrasted strangely with the innocent and charming good looks of the flaxen-haired blue-eyed Roumanian girl educator in charge of the children. Indeed I often noticed on my Youth Aliyah journeys the contrast between teachers of the most idealist type with those who seemed there for some quite other reason.

The slender, shyly smiling, Roumanian girl, although extremely timid, appeared to have the children well in hand. Tea consisted of great hunks of coarse bread spread very thinly with a jam-like substance—which was not jam. Some of the children seemed very hungry and pretended they had eaten nothing in order to get more bread. After tea the children were encouraged to dance, which they did, though apathetically I thought.

I kept asking myself: "Are these children happy?" It is easy
for a visitor, full of sympathy for the Jewish State, and greeted
by smiling faces of children with whom he has no real contact,
to imagine that they are as contented as he would wish them
to be. But if he asks himself "Would I be happy if, as a child,
I had been taken from my home and parents and sent across
the sea to an impoverished country known in the sacred
writings as the Promised Land, where after a few weeks spent
in a Sorting Out Centre I was directed to some other institution
chosen for me according to the supposed qualifications of my
political and religious background?" The answer would hardly
be an unqualified Yes. Nor would it necessarily be an unqualified No. To put myself in the place of these children I have to
understand something of the miserable conditions from which
they have come and compare these with the rather better circumstances of the Youth Aliyah centres. On the whole a great
many of the children are better off in the Kibbutzim and
Children's Villages than they would be in the ma'abara with
their parents. They grow conscious of this themselves and are
unhappy when they are asked to return to their old life. Moreover Israel does more than any other nation for its children.
In a very real sense the country has become the parent of those
who for one reason or another have been taken from their homes.

Yet if I had visited a Sorting Out Centre in 1935 or 1939, I
do not think I would have felt even such doubts about the
happiness of the children. For the first young immigrants were
Zionists of the kind who have become the ruling class in Israel.
They arrived already convinced of the philosophic necessity of
cultivating the soil of Palestine. The Eastern children arrive
without any such conviction, and the educators are as much
puzzled by them, as are the children by the Promised Land
which turns out so different from the Paradise of their belief.

Back at Haifa we walked through the main streets. Those
shops which had windows packed with goods were selling use-

less objects like silver ornaments, beads and leatherwork. Other shop-windows had the gaping, bare, soiled emptiness of the shops in cities which have been at war. One or two things I had forgotten to bring and had to buy. I paid I£2 for the cheapest nail scissors I could find, I£1 for a nail-brush. Even at the present rate of exchange this is expensive.

I made some inquiries, and arrived at the following rough estimates about prices and living conditions in Israel in the spring of 1952:—

Bread is unrationed, but expensive. The ration of tea and of very poor coffee is about 4 ounces of each per person a week.

Meat is almost unobtainable: a small ration is perhaps distributed once every three months.

Frozen fish—always the same variety of cod—is obtainable. Tinned fish has disappeared from the shops. There are no sardines.

Milk is obtainable.

There are about enough potatoes to serve them with two meals a week per family.

Oranges and citreous fruit rejected by the export market can be bought during the three months of the fruit season.

There are very few green vegetables.

Noodles, formerly easy to get, are now rationed.

Porridge is obtainable.

The allowance of flour amounts to a ½-kilo. each month per head.

There are special rations for undernourished children.

In the Kibbutzim, the food position is better than in the towns, as happens always in the country.

Food assignments coming to Youth Aliyah, contributed by people in America and other countries, are distributed according to need.

Youth Aliyah children enjoy about 50 per cent. more rations than other children.

For most Orientals this diet is a great deal superior to any-

5. (*above*) Interest in art is encouraged

6. A young craftsman enjoys his training

7. The Sephardi children who
   want to be individuals

8. Roadside child from the Yemen

9. Neoth Mordechai: Balu carries the
   future of Kibbutz

thing to which they are accustomed in their own countries. This has the result that a great many of them turn over their rations to the Black Market.

The scale of prices on the Black Market is indicated by these approximate "quotations":—

Coffee, I£8 per kilo.

Meat, I£6 per kilo.

One chicken, I£10.

These figures are noted in my diary on March 21st, 1952. They are certainly quite different now, and were probably disputable at the time.

Statistics usually mean little to me but these figures do convey the impression of what it felt like to be in Israel, and I quote them for that reason. Conditions for nearly everyone I met, except those lucky people who received food parcels from America, were really bad. My general impression is that the friends I met in Israel were about four times worse off than my friends in England. Without meat, and with only the most tasteless kind of fish, their diet completely lacked variety. They lived their personal lives in an inflation far worse than ours. To me, it appears that we in England often exaggerate in describing our own austerity. But austerity is real in Israel, and as the food in restaurants and hotels showed, there is no escaping it.

Everywhere in the lives of the people I met I saw reflections of the condition of Israel itself, a country whose imports exceed her exports by at least five times.

Real austerity, coupled with the existence of a Black Market and a public economy on the verge of a catastrophe only averted by the generosity of American Jewry, makes a foggy and depressing mental climate. Like some socialists in England after the war, the Israelis courageously try not to think about the effect of lowered material standards on spiritual values. The highest values of the few thousand people whose example still shines through the land, are remarkably unaffected. But there are values almost as important, if of a slightly lower order, which are also spiritual. For example, art, entertainment, amusement even. What I saw of these I found to suffer simply from the lack of energy-giving life which is necessary for painting, the theatre, and music.

The post-war atmosphere of Jerusalem, Haifa and Tel Aviv, with bomb-damaged houses and shop-windows empty of all but ornaments on sale for tourists or clothes scarcely obtainable for Israelis even with ration coupons, demonstrates that for the Jews coming out of a Europe damaged but still with far higher standards than this, Israel is an end of something as well as a beginning. For a great many, it must seem like the last bomb that has fallen, robbing them of everything but their lives. Bombed Warsaw, bombed Berlin, as well as the Displaced Persons' Camp, and even the barbed wire of Auschwitz, are enormous ghosts, shades of the universal ghetto which crossed the ocean too and reached the shores of the Promised Land.

CHAPTER III

ARRIVAL AT JERUSALEM

M R. MELITZ fetched me from the grey stone hotel of
Weimar Republican rectangles, with its gardens of shrubs
and flowering trees, and we drove to Jerusalem. As we left
Haifa along the coastal road, he continued to act as my mentor
and resisted my tendency to fall into a green trance of watching
the landscape unreel on either side through the glossy wind-
screen of the car. Outside Haifa on the flat strip of coast between
the Mediterranean and the Carmel range we passed two extensive hut-covered areas. Melitz explained that the first of
these was the encampment to which the immigrants are sent
the day after their arrival in Israel. Here they are interviewed,
medically examined, and so on. If discovered to be fit, they are
then sent to the second lot of huts which constitutes the first
ma'abara one sees after entering Israel. The ma'abara, I discovered, could be better than the rather ramshackle encampment I now saw; they could also be far worse. They could
consist of tin huts or ragged tents or patched up box-like
dwellings not much better than the terrible slums along the
coast on the outskirts of Bombay.

The immigrants, Melitz continued, stay for a period of
anything up to two years at the ma'abara. During this period
of initiation, they are expected to become self-sufficient. They
work on agricultural projects, tree-planting, pipe-laying, road
building—all the projects which make Israel seem not one of
the oldest landscapes in the world, but like a pioneer country
which has just been occupied by an army with advanced ideas.

So we drove on. On our left was the ma'abara, a kind of transported slum, whose occupants were busy taking stones out of the soil and putting in trees and pipes; on our right the soft, blurred Mediterranean—fields and fields of powder-blue-grey cornflowers, scarcely disturbing the deeper more transparent blue of the sky.

First of all I was interested in the facts I was being told, then I became interested in Mr. Melitz' own attitude. It reached really a great deal further than what we saw. The landscape to him was not just being cleared of rocks and planted. It was bound to yield oil sooner or later, and more water than anyone had dreamed of. He said, in so many words: "I am sure we will find everything we need, sooner or later." He believed in the miracle of Moses striking water from the rock. That hundreds of people think and feel like Mr. Melitz is an important fact about Israel.

Between Haifa and Jerusalem we saw much evidence of the work being done by the immigrants. On the desert-like strip of sand-dunes further south along the coast, branches were being laid on the sand to anchor it down, coarse shrubs and trees were being planted. On the roadside edge near a marshy area, large whitish-coloured roots of eucalyptus were awaiting plantation. Their tubers draw up the water, and in this way malarial swamps have been drained. At another place where there were rocky hills, the stones having been taken away so as to reveal fields of fresh soil underneath, were being used to terrace the hillside. On the plains between the sea and the hills of Jerusalem, new settlements were springing up, walls being erected, trenches dug and pipes laid. All this was being done with a recklessness which had a certain gaiety, for new-cut sappy wood, and fresh-tarred black pipes look slick and gleaming. But it also promised a great deal of ugliness for the future; unless, indeed, these housing schemes were as temporary as, say, the prefabricated settlements in bomb-damaged areas of English towns.

Melitz went on telling me things. The immigrant after a couple of years or so, graduates from the ma'abara to his own house. The government—he said—has been wise and imaginative in arranging that often the new settlements are built side by side with the ma'abara, so that the rather depressed immigrants can see their new homes being constructed in front of their eyes, and can even assist in building them.

Our journey from Haifa to Jerusalem, which lasted only about four hours, showed us a great variety of landscape: the beautiful hills of Carmel with their waving green slopes surmounted by castellated reddish rock; then the sand-dune-desert stretch of coast; then the rich citreous groves of orange and lemon trees, enclosed by rows of cypresses looking like ancient crumbling walls around gardens; and then the long narrow neck of land between Caesarea and Tel Aviv, where you see the Mediterranean to the west, the flowing hills of Transjordan to the east. Many a time—Mr. Melitz told me—the wanderlusting young Israelis on their excursions have accidentally strayed across the border here, and been captured by the Arabs.

In the mind of an inhabitant of a small country the beauty of home lies in his ability to imagine vividly his native landscape, to animate his mental map with fields and hills and trees. The pleasure is all the greater if the simple picture in his mind of his land is also a very variegated one.

From the strategic point of view, Israel is rather unfortunate. It suggests an attenuated insect with one extremity widely separated from the other by a slender abdomen which seems to invite an enemy to sever it. But to the home-loving sentimentalist, it is hour-glass-shaped, with the sand falling as it were away from the beautiful Galilean hills, through the narrow funnel of the map between Caesarea and Tel Aviv, down to the bottom sand-filled part of the hour-glass which is the Negev desert.

This image I only set up, to pull it down again, remembering the eastwards camel's head part of the map in which Jerusalem juts into Transjordan. But the point is that there is pleasure in thinking of such shapes—the pleasure of the inhabitant of a small country.

And the Israelis acquired a passionate love for Palestine very early on. After the establishment of the State, hitch-hiking became a craze. Everyone wanted to see the country which was "all ours"—to use the words of Isvi Feigenbaum.

So all in a morning we passed from the Carmel hills near Haifa, through the country of orange groves, along the narrow coastline strip of waving cornlands, and then Eastwards towards Jerusalem.

The terraced hills round Jerusalem, rise one behind another, tier on tier, rather flat-looking against the sky like the Step-pyramid. Then the road curves round between the two final hills, and on the skyline you see the first houses of Jerusalem looking rather like packing cases. Although this first view is very much like seeing a stage set from the back, it does not detract from the convincing sensation that Jerusalem is the summit of this part of the world.

At the bend in the road where you first see in the distance the untidy box-buildings of the literally New Jerusalem, you see also the remains of an old Arab village. It lies opposite you on the other side of a valley, immediately below Jerusalem, which is two ranges of hills away. From here the new part of the City seems all angles and assertiveness, the Arab village grows on the near hill-side like barnacles on a rock; barnacles which have now been fragmented and broken away, the life torn out, but still having the tenacious force of their suitability to the landscape.

In my journeys through Israel I saw many ruined Arab villages, often much more destroyed than this one. Very little was said about them by my guides, but they always gave me the feeling that in their ruin they looked permanent, whilst in their triumph the settlements and town quarters built by the Jews looked precarious and temporary.

We drove to what I suppose is the centre of the new part of
Jerusalem, the King David's Hotel. From my room on the
third floor, I looked over the moat-like valley which divides the
new from the old city. From here the wall of the Old City,
silhouetted against the sky, seemed a bristling fence of turrets
and spires, a battery aimed at the highest imaginable heaven.
Spires, crosses, minaretes, domes and the city wall of the hymn
"There is a green hill far away," seem to stand at the top of a
precipice which you look up to from underneath, making their
assaults on several different Gods. This spectacle gave me a
feeling of respect mixed with sadness that the most holy city
should yet demonstrate the world's failure to achieve spiritual
unity. It is here that three great religions, and the innumerable
sects into which these religions are divided, have tried to
materialize their meanings in shrines and monuments. The
total effect resembles too much the staking out of rival claims
on land where there is supposed to be gold. There are grotesque
collidings of spiritual forces. Rocks and tombs unite within
themselves conflicting symbolic meanings of Christ, Mahomed
and David, like those reflecting photographs which looked at
from one angle show quite a different picture from that seen at
another one. The place sacred to one creed is the object of
vilification by another equally claiming a monopoly of truth.

There is no easy solution of the problem of spiritual conflict
petrified in the stones of Jerusalem. If partisans of fundamentally opposed creeds believe that they know the truth about the
most important values in this world and the next, then there is
something even more materialistic about the compromises they
make (in order to recognize each other's claims to eternal
knowledge) than in battling to the death for a creed. For if you
know the truth—and if all the handed-down sacred writings
prove it to you—how can you come to any compromise with
an opponent who believes that you are wrong and damned for
it, except on the basis of an implicit understanding that you
and he have both ceased to believe in the authority of your

divine texts? Religions are the justification of wars because they maintain truths which lie beyond death, and the ultimate proof that you believe in these truths is that you can die for them.

In our time this may be taking the logic of belief too far, because the nature of war has itself changed. All the same there is something shabby about the modern compromise, and to see all the houses of God side by side in Jerusalem is to have a Samuel Butlerish vision of the musical Banks of a meta-physical Wall Street or "the City." One begins almost to respect the hatred between Arab and Jew. If they cannot love one another, perhaps that is the best way in which each can retain his spiritual identity.

I do not mean that Jerusalem proves the folly of the creeds. On the contrary, it shows the tremendous force of the spiritual life of several great religions which have all emerged from this part of the world. Religious hatred is the inevitable result of the lack of a universal religion; yet it is impossible to imagine all men accepting one creed. Since there are many, one must admire men for clinging passionately to their separate beliefs. That they have killed and died for them is tragic, but it is not foolish. Or if there is some level of reality where the mutual destructiveness of the religious appears but a farce, then this is only because perhaps all human conflicts even when they lead to tragedies, are in some sense farcical.

Every religion which has gained a hold over the minds of large numbers of men has done so through the religious ex-pressing their ideas in concrete symbols accessible to the minds of ordinary people. Perhaps the religious tragedies are the result of this zeal for expressing spiritual truths in a very literal way. The idea of having "Holy Places" demonstrates the passion for actually possessing objects which have become symbols. But this possessiveness no more invalidates the idea of the sacred which the "Holy Place" symbolizes than does the possessiveness of a lover of beauty for a beautiful painting discredit the judgment which makes him desire the painting.

So Jerusalem remains Holy despite the ravages wreaked on her by men's passion to possess the symbols of the divine.

All the same, Jerusalem is forbidding. It combines beauty with ugliness, antiquity with the frightful gaffes of the 19th and 20th Century Christian and Jewish architects. The rocks are old, but even the buildings of the Old City only go back to the Middle Ages. It seems to say to all the religious who have tried to possess it: "Wishing to possess me, you lose me. I break to pieces in your hands."

This is even true to-day with the Israelis. For Jerusalem is the goal which the Jews have won; it is also the place from which they are shut out, since in gaining it they have been excluded from the Old City.

Jerusalem is a perpetual reminder of the paradoxical nature of the Jewish State.

Fundamentally this paradox rests on the fact that the Jewish State is an attempt to turn a negative situation into a positive one, and everything appertaining to the Jews for the past two thousand years into its opposite. Israel has the mentality of the land, the Diaspora of the ghetto.

The idea of Israel is that the Jews who are now there will move, as it were, in the reverse direction to that in which they had previously been going. This is the reassuring aspect of the paradox. The terrifying aspect is that the Jews may find that to themselves they have ceased to be Jews.

For the immense majority of Jews, being Jewish has meant being in exile, being a minority, being persecuted, being shut in the ghetto; living a life, and having a mentality which goes with these things. It has meant pursuing the occupations which have been permitted to the Jew by the Gentiles, and developing the cerebral attitudes and intense inner life of those who did not belong to the life around them, were cut off from a dynamic relationship with the soil, because they were not of the land on which they lived.

The early Jewish immigrants from Russia, Poland and Germany realized this fundamental difference between the Jews of the ghetto and the Jews in Palestine. Their whole conception of the National Home was that it should provide the conditions for the emergence of a Jewry the opposite of that in the Diaspora.

The idea of making a Jew who was not a Jew—or who was no one's idea of an existing one—is itself paradoxical. Yet it is perfectly consistent with the concept of the exile as the negation of the life of the Ingathering. The idea was to produce a positive Jew—and the Jews on the Kibbutzim did that. They produced Jews who prided themselves on not looking like Jews. How often people in Israel boasted to me that their children have blue eyes, fair hair and snub noses!

But to-day there is another kind of paradox, of a disquieting kind. This might be called the paradox of the Ingathering; that if you release all the Jews coming from every country of the world from the negative consciousness of being Jewish, then the assembled Jews discover that they really never had anything in common except their persecution. The Jew is now his own opposite in quite another sense. Having returned to Israel he discovers that he is not a Jew—or that if he is a Jew, these other people aren't. He has far more in common with the people of the country he has come from than with these others. What could be more different than a German Jew from a Yemenite Jew?

It is the nature of Israel to produce paradoxical situations, and to resolve so many contradictions, one has to think of constructive paradoxes instead of destructive ones. The most nihilistic one would be to discover that the Jews are only united as a race when they are in exile and living among people who tell them (reassuringly as it turns out) that they are Jews. Somehow the gentile myth of the Jew—with the sting taken out of its tail—has to be transported to Israel so that Poles and Russians and Iraquians and Yemenites can live together, all reflecting that they are Jews. Thus I recently saw an article in which the idea of the Exile was transferred to Israel. "It is said," the writer argued, "that for 2,000 years the Jews have been in exile and have been united in their consciousness by virtue of this overwhelming common factor of their highly various situation. From this it has also been deduced by some Jewish anti-Zionists, that without the Exile the widely separated Jews have nothing in common. But this is quite wrong. For, strictly speaking, the Jews in Israel are in exile from the Exile. After all," he goes on (I paraphrase his ideas from memory), "they have been driven to Israel as the result of the persecution which exists at all other places always." For it is dogma among zealous Zionists that the Jews not only are and have been, but are inevitably bound always to be persecuted in the Diaspora, and that any other idea is only an illusion.

When I first read this argument, it struck me as comic. But, on reflection, I think it contains a measure of truth. Israel is largely the consequence of the persecution of the Jews. A great many of the people living there are in fact doing so because they are in exile. If they discover that they have few positive qualities in common with other Jews, it is well to remember that the factor of exile still exists, and justifies their presence in Israel.

But "the exile from the Exile" is a negative conception, and in a later chapter, I shall try to suggest a way of looking at Israel which is more positive.

Since the Arabs occupy the Old City, and no visitor with an Israeli visa is allowed into Arab territory, I could not see the most beautiful part of Jerusalem. The modern part, built since 1858, makes a separate town. Spread out over the hills and consisting of areas separated by big gaps of unbuilt-on land, it resembles a collection of suburbs with no centre. Even that which more than any other section should perhaps be the centre—the road which has on the one side the great tower of the Y.M.C.A. building, and on the other, the barrack-like King David's Hotel—adjoins a heath-like stretch of waste land with olive trees and shrubby plants growing on it.

Devastation caused by the fighting has added to the bald patches of the new city. It is difficult for the visitor to-day to distinguish between what has been destroyed and what has never been built.

If Jerusalem had the appearance of a 19th Century town, its disorder and incompleteness would not be so surprising. But owing to a rule (recently relaxed) that every house must be built from the local stone from the surrounding hills, the architecture has a certain uniformity of appearance. It consists for the most part of unattractive buildings made out of beautiful material so that the whole effect is not ugly, though many of the details may be.

From my bedroom window I certainly had a picture of the City which was far from being ugly. Immediately below my window, there was a screen of cypress trees with the column of one palm tree in their midst, bursting rocket-like at the apex into a shower of plume-like leaves. On the further side of the moat-like valley—with wrecks of houses from the time when it was No Man's Land during the war—were the mediaeval walls and buttresses, which held the Old City packed within them as in a box. Domes and towers and waving tops of cypresses emerged above like nodding plumes of helmets. To the extreme right of this wall I saw the Domitian Church with its squat tower surmounted by its triangular roof. Beyond and behind the walls of the City to the left of my view, Mount Scopus culminated in the needle-like tower of the Church of the Ascension.

The whole wide profile of the hillside bearing the Old City, stood out in a single piece like a ship against the wave-like lines of the distant hills of Judaea.

From my window this view changed every minute of the day. In the early morning it hit the eyes with bright contrasted patches of dark cypresses, and walls and the hillside reflecting the intense light. In the evening it gradually became absorbed into a total stony greyness, as though the walls of the Old City had roots which drew the colour up out of the grass. The most beautiful hour was doubtless sunset, when the walls gleamed an enamel flame-like colour, a thickset band of fire between the hills and the sky. Later the walls faded and the sky was painted with greens and purples which in turn expired, to be succeeded by the sensational black and white of night and stars.

The sky seems immense at Jerusalem, as though the irregular silhouette of the Old City were at the bottom of a canvas three-quarters sky. The grey uniformity of the stony city makes one aware of it during the day as though Jerusalem were a stony floor under a well of light. After sunset there is such a vivid mixing of colours that you find yourself looking at a great stretch of sky in the endeavour to relate the greenish glow above the hills to the blues and purples overhead. And at night the spires—even the great tower of the Y.M.C.A. building becomes solemn and beautiful—point to the stars.

The sky above Jerusalem seems animated with magic figures. It is a sky painted by Marc Chagall who is, in fact, a Jewish painter who did not visit Jerusalem until 1951. But his paintings in which figures, animals and houses seem dreaming on the earth below a vividly peopled sky, wonderfully suggest the city.

On my arrival in Jerusalem, I was taken over by an American lady. Mrs. Y——, although not Jewish, had married an Israeli, and was living in Jerusalem. She took me round the book-shops, where we found that as a result of the currency restrictions, there were very few foreign books, and none at all that were recently published. The only books were paper-bound editions on such subjects as How to Keep a Fruit Garden, or Hop

Farming in Kent. Mrs. Y—— was enthusiastic about Jerusalem.
With straight features, and hair pressed flat against the back
of her head and ending in curls at the base of her neck, she
marched through the streets like a banner, saying that her
friends in America couldn't and wouldn't ever understand the
way she felt, they thought she was crazy ever to have left New
York, they couldn't understand why she didn't think that
refrigerators and T-stakes were the most important things in
life, but she didn't mind about the discomforts and incon-
veniences, she felt something about Jerusalem that she couldn't
explain, but it was the first thing she wanted to explain to
everyone she met, and she had never felt anything like it ever
anywhere before.

We came to a part of the City she particularly liked, on a
ledge above the No Man's Land below the Old City wall.
Mrs. Y—— told me that this was a dangerous place to be,
because Arab sentries occasionally picked off a Jew or two
from here, especially at night. Most of the houses here were
little better than ruins, and they were supposed to have been
evacuated by order of the authorities. In fact, though, a
great many people were living here, leading a life reminiscent
of a modernistic stage set for a play by Gorki I had once seen
in which one side was torn from a tenement building in order
to reveal three storeys of misery going on underneath. These
people, Mrs. Y—— explained, were members of a ma'abara
that had gone bankrupt. They had occupied these buildings
despite the official governmental ban on them. They were
"squatters."

In their wretched rags of clothes, with their few pieces of
furniture in their hollowed-out dwellings, they certainly looked
as badly off as anyone I have seen anywhere. They were, of
course, the "Orientals." They were my first sight of the
seeping-in of the terrible African and Asiatic poverty into the
Jewish State.

We went on further to a street of smaller houses perched

against the steep hill-side, where children were gathering the weeds around the houses, and—rather to our surprise—eating them then and there. Whether they did this because these plants were delectable or because they—the children—were very hungry, we couldn't make out.

We looked across at the ramparts of the Old City—about half a mile away from us at this point, I supposed—and had the satisfaction of discerning, in a watch tower, a dark figure who was unquestionably a Moroccan sentry.

That afternoon, Melitz took me to a ma'abara on the outskirts of the City. It was like a small town consisting of several streets, with a mud track as broad as a main road running down the centre of it. At the edge of this place, there was still some green grass where people cultivated small gardens round their huts and kept chickens. Towards the centre there was no greenery, and the square, which was the hub of the place, was nothing more than a large patch of dried mud. There was a stench—not so strong—but distinctly reminiscent of the smell on the outskirts of Bombay. In the centre of the settlement was a market place run by some antique women, and some old men with grey beards, looking like Druses, who sat on the mud pavement, selling things. They had transported the atmosphere of Morocco here. Some of the huts had their doors opened and inside I could see shops with vegetables, eggs, fruit, cakes and bread—better than any I had seen in Jerusalem.

Through the open door of another hut I saw a large coloured photograph of King George VI and a garish advertisement for some brand of English cigarette. I thought the large florid-looking owner, with her mass of tousled hair, might just possibly have come from Whitechapel. However, she spoke only Arabic. When Mr. Melitz asked her whether we might go into her hut and look round (not that there was anything which we couldn't see from where we were standing) she simply replied in her Arabic dialect—"I have not," an answer which didn't seem to take us anywhere.

There were quite a few young men and boys walking about this place wearing pyjamas. That they do this really horrifies the Israelis, because the idea that pyjamas are chic day-time garb is a particularly Arab one.

In the street, a French-speaking Moroccan boy, who had a certain languid grace and an air of superiority, greeted Melitz. He wore a blue pin-stripe suit, with open-necked shirt. He offered us cigarettes, and as he lit mine a large ring on his fore-finger flashed under my eyes. He explained that he had been in the Youth Aliyah Centre, but had left on account of the arrival of his parents in Israel. He was now keeping his parents in a small house which contained eight other people. He said—with a gesture—that although he was proud to support his family, he regretted every day he was not with Youth Aliyah. "Are your parents here in the ma'abara?" I asked. "Oh no," he answered, looking round disdainfully. "I am here just as a tourist."

"Not one of our best products," Mr. Melitz commented as we walked away. "You see," he continued, "I am going to show you the worst as well as the best, while you are in Israel. This is one of the worst places we have in the country. Places like this are the result of the tremendous pressure of a population which has increased by three-quarters of a million, thus doubling itself, in the past three or four years."

10. Yemenites of the Ma'abara

11. Pet adopted by the children of Neza Buchenwald

12. Best African cooking in the Negev desert

13. The Yemenite Witch doctor and his patient

CHAPTER IV

THE DISTURBED AND THE DISTURBING

SAINT SIMON, in the neighbourhood of Jerusalem, was the first of the children's villages which I saw: an untidy, sprawling place on a stone-covered slope overlooking a valley, beyond which lies Arab territory.

At the entrance, an office where we met the "educator"; an almost white-haired, young-looking man, with lean, lined, sallow face out of which looked keenly interested eyes. He had an expression of alertness and kindness which I came to associate with most Youth Aliyah educators.

On his desk were various specimens of pottery with pleasant primitive designs, needle-work and carvings of animals made out of olive wood. All these were of a higher quality than those I had seen in the Sorting Out Centre, and I discovered that Saint Simon specialized in the arts. He told me that the carvings, which showed much feeling for animals, were done by North African children.

This settlement has been in existence since 1949. It contains 190 children, coming from 29 different countries.

When the educator first came here, he was struck by the difference of attitude between the children of each of the different countries. Later, he noticed more and more how the children came to resemble one another, until it was not easy to tell where each came from.

The children here concentrated mostly on their art-work, but they also cultivated the grounds. As we went out of the office into the open air, we saw evidence of this: patches of freshly turned earth planted with small trees; and flowers which blossomed out of what had been barren soil. But the greater part of the land remained unredeemed, and with its many protruding stones deeply embedded, it seemed that the soil was only a thin covering over a horny underground armature of solid stone.

The children, he observed, were bored by having to move the stones. It was tedious and heavy work, and it took them a whole day to clear a few metres of land.

Children, with their small hands, spending a whole day in clearing enough space to put in a few plants! There is a great deal of Israel in that picture, I thought, looking at the heartbreaking miles of stony soil which filled most of the landscape in every direction as far as the eye could see, and the wonderful gash of raw soil, potent as blood, in which the plants grew. Beyond the settlement, just over the hill, lay the Arab territory, and that was the completing touch which made this landscape typical.

On the path by our side was a Chinese girl with oval face, almond-shaped eyes and a cool, clear expression of her smiling mouth. She walked arm in arm with a Bulgarian girl and a Turkish boy. The three of them looked like brother and sisters.

We went to the potting shed, where a 12-year-old Roumanian showed us the work in progress. In the schoolroom a play was being rehearsed by children from a dozen different countries.

On the following day, I went to Ein Karem, west of Jerusalem, to see my second children's village. This is one of the most charming places in this part of the country.

The village climbs up the sides of a valley between rows of cypresses. The valley is full of olive trees and flowering trees of many kinds. It reminded me of the beautiful olive slopes and cypresses at the monastery of Daphne near Athens.

On top of the hills at either side of the valley are Italian, Greek orthodox and French monasteries.

According to Mrs. Y——, who accompanied me here, the fountain in the village is where John the Baptist is supposed to have been baptized. Baedeker (1922) maintains "the tradition which assigns to this spot the birthplace of John the Baptist is of no great antiquity." It then goes on to associate the well with the "supposed visit of the Virgin," causing it to be called Mary's well. Marmorosch's *Old and New Places in Palestine, Syria and Lebanon* says that the home of Zacharias and Elizabeth, St. John the Baptist's parents, stands on the site of the present Church of St. John in the Franciscan Monastery of St. John.

Mrs. Y—— told me another story, more easily confirmed, about the Youth Aliyah village here. One of the children interested himself, it seems, in botanical specimens. He was encouraged, and soon showed himself to have great talents as a collector. The Children's Village has a room put aside devoted to displaying his collection.

A girl educator showed us round the school, which was mostly of Persian and Turkish children. The rooms were simple and bare with stone floors. There were four beds to a room, each bed alongside a wall. The only decorations were drawings done by the children. The most striking of these were by a boy who copies coloured prints from advertisements, cigarette cards and the like. Although he has real gifts for drawing and painting, he refuses—the educator told me—to draw in any other way. This, he says, is the way in which he learned to draw in Turkey. I noticed, though, that he added different colours to the prints which he copied and somehow contrived to turn them into something charming and original.

The children we met here—especially the girls—seemed both shy and open, in the way which often makes Italian peasants attractive. They seemed to have brought to Israel a primitive attitude which had blossomed in the atmosphere of affection with which, in this particular place, they were surrounded. I was to feel less optimistic about the success of the Oriental children later on.

The third of the places for children which I visited in the neighbourhood of Jerusalem, was the so-called Swiss village, in the hills not far from Ein Karem. Paid for by Swiss funds, and in fact quite like a Swiss village, with its châlet-like huts under fir trees, it is a cool, green paradise among the hills. The village seems a garden with summer houses in it, with views between boughs of the surrounding hills.

This paradisal atmosphere is perhaps a bit deceptive, for the children here are those who have come out of various hells. They are those children whom the educators have regarded as disturbed, with the result that they have been weeded out of the Kibbutzim and the Children's Institutions, and sent here for special surveyance. Most of them have terrible backgrounds of war, revolution, prison and concentration camp. Many have seen their parents killed in front of their eyes, or have spent weeks wandering through Siberia or Eastern Europe.

I was met by the educator, Moses ——, a proud, sensitive, intelligent-looking young man, whose dark hair seemed to grow bird-like in three large feathers folding back across the sides and the top of his head. His face had the lines of someone who has lived much out of doors, watching living beings very keenly.

Before going to meet the children, I asked him to tell me by what criteria they were considered "maladjusted." He answered, "Maladjusted doesn't mean that they are stupid. Some are more intelligent than the other children in the places they come from. What they have most in common is perhaps the problems of terrible pasts. Most have grown up without their parents since the age of four."

The main symptoms which have resulted in the children being sent here, are aggressiveness, nervous habits, stammering, and the inability to co-operate with others.

Only the most difficult cases are given individual psycho-analytic treatment. The most usual treatment is by "group analysis," that is, by a group of between six and 15 children being formed and then encouraged to discuss their problems.

The children are also given certain games to play as a form of therapy. Moses showed us one of these games. It consisted of a miniature theatre with a proscenium into which the child could slip any one of a number of scenes painted on cardboard, together with a stage where he could make characters chosen from a number of cardboard figures enact a drama. The backgrounds were stereotyped scenes: a forest, the sea, a domestic interior, a battlefield, a church or synagogue, etc. Having decided on the scenery of his story, the child picks one of the stereotyped cardboard figures—handsome hero, beautiful heroine, priest, devil, villain, soldier, policeman, thug, doctor, wounded man, father, mother, corpse. I noticed that a nude "cutie" was one of the possible protagonists.

Here is an example of such a drama enacted by a child. It is the story of a Greek girl, called Rina, aged 10½.

Before Rina came to the Swiss village she was in one of the settlements to which the children are ordinarily sent. The educators there felt unable to cope with her on account of her habit of bursting into tears, and having fits of uncontrollable screaming. They said that she was never quiet.

She came to Israel from Greece. Apart from this, nothing was known about her, and the educators found it impossible to get her to tell them anything. She remembered nothing whatever before the moment that she arrived at Haifa. Apparently she knew no Greek and could speak only Hebrew.

She was asked to play the game with the toy theatre. Immediately she chose the bedroom scene, and acted out the following story.

"There was once a big girl who wept a great deal when she was at home. A man suddenly came into the room, and said: 'Why do you weep, beautiful girl?' She answered 'I weep because my mother has gone away, and has never returned.' The man said to her: 'Don't weep. For until your mother returns, you can remain with me.'

"She stayed several days with the man. One day the mother came back and did not recognize the girl. The mother looked and looked at the girl and yet she did not find her."

At this point, Moses broke off and interpolated: "When Rina told this part of the story, she took the figure who represented the mother and made it walk round and round the one who represented the girl, always with her back to the girl, and not seeing her."

He continued the story in her words:

"Then the mother went out of the house, and sat on a stone, and began to weep. Then the girl was glad. She ran out and said to the mother: 'I am your child'. And both went home."

"This was the story," said Moses. I asked her then: 'What does the idea of the beautiful girl convey to you?'

"She answered: 'It is I myself. I was always a beautiful girl.'

"Then I asked her: 'What does the idea of the man who found you alone in the house, weeping, convey to you?'

"That," she said, "was our neighbour." Then suddenly she burst into tears.

"I know now," she said. "It was in the night, and I screamed. Then our neighbour came to me."

"I asked: 'Who is your neighbour?' She avoided answering this question, and continued: 'I was alone at night, and the neighbour came only in the morning'—she corrected what she had said before—'When the mother and father had gone away.'

"Then she re-told the whole story. 'When I was a little child, very small, one night I woke up, and I have never seen my parents since that night. I screamed terribly until the morning, and a neighbour came who took me to a Red Cross tent. Before this, I had, when I was very small, thought all men to be like my father. Now no more.'

"We managed," continued Moses, "to trace her mother's address to Canada. We wrote to the mother and discovered what had really happened. The father had been killed in the Greek fighting, and the mother had run away with a Canadian

14. The terraced hills near Jerusalem

15. The Lake of Tiberias at Ein Geb

16. The new ideal home of the Kibbutz at Neoth Mordechai

17. The tree-cool children's village of Ben Shemen

soldier. A neighbour had rescued the girl and taken her to the Red Cross, who conveyed her to Youth Aliyah.

"When we told the girl she had a mother," Moses said, "She had one of her worst attacks of screaming and crying. 'Must I be taken away from her?' she had cried."

After this, Moses took us to the dining room where all the children were having their tea. The children burst into loud cries of "Schalom, schalom," welcoming us. Another educator, a tall fair-haired young man, got up and explained in Hebrew what was meant by a "writer." Then Moses read a story, which was about the fighting in the recent war.

The atmosphere was very tense throughout the reading. Moses who read the story in what seemed a rather dramatic way, was as conscious of his audience as is the conductor of an orchestra. It was a difficult orchestra too, in which some of the musicians refused to play. One of the girls buried her head in her hands and giggled hysterically throughout most of the reading, and some of the boys were whispering to each other. Twice Moses adopted the tactics of stopping the reading and simply looking at the interrupter, until he or she had recovered. But most of the children listened attentively.

We went back to his room with Moses, and he showed us some of the children's drawings, which are used as part of their analysis. One of them was of four figures on a gallows. It was by a boy who had seen all his family hanged.

The visit to the Swiss village illustrated for me the terrible background from which so many of these children have come. Children who have seen their parents killed in front of their eyes; children sent to concentration camps in Germany; children treated as pariahs in Vienna, slinking about the streets and "forbidden to enter a public garden"; children all of whose relations have disappeared utterly off the face of the earth; children who have wandered like animals over plains and forests, hunting for food; children who have become members of the gangs in Casablanca and Beirut: the pasts of these children in Israel form an immense catalogue, a directory of the crimes of the adults against the children in our time.

Not just the Germans—the whole civilized world is involved in the pasts of these children. The English, who accepted a policy of shutting them out of Palestine when many might have been saved, bear a special responsibility. There is a point where Hitlerism involves all our civilization in guilt, and that is in the failure of "the West" to save these victims.

Israel is doing something to redeem our civilization in saving these children, and just as the guilt for their sufferings goes beyond Fascism, so surely the duty to help them goes beyond Israel, and Israel should be helped in helping them. The children are Israel's, but they are the responsibility of the world.

In writing about the children in this book, I am often conscious that I am writing about something else. For the situation of the children crystallizes many of the problems of Israel itself in relation to the conscience of the rest of the world.

Looked at in one way, Israel is a small country consisting of Jews who have chosen to go there and who, by doing so, have acquired national independence. Looked at in another way, it is the result of the persecution of the Jews in this century, unprecedented in scale, and the welfare of the new State should be a question of moral conscience for the whole world.

Even those who are not directly responsible for the excesses of anti-semitism, are now to some degree responsible for seeing that Israel does not become the ghetto of the world. If the crimes against the Jews are not laid against the doors of Christians, the opportunity to atone for a world crime now is. To the Jews Israel is the national home; but to the rest of the world it is redemption for century-long anti-semitism which has reached a climax of horror in our generation.

This visit also left me curious about the psychology of the "difficult" children. A few days later I went to interview Dr. Dux, Director of B'nai Brith Home for Maladjusted Children.

I wished to find out more about the difference between the Oriental and the Western children.

Dr. Dux said that one of the difficulties in dealing with the children coming from Morocco, Tunis, Iraq, the Yemen, and so on, was that the psychological tests used with the Westerners did not apply to them.

"If you examine a Western child," he said, "he has at the back of his mind a certain concept of ordered knowledge to which he relates his own intelligence, without his realizing that he is doing so. But this relating of his own intellect to a scaffolding of intellectual order behind it, does not arise with the Oriental child.

"Thus it happens that sometimes some of the Oriental children come to Israel having received shocks early on in their lives, which we are not able to detect with our tests, and which block all their responses more completely than would be the case with the Western child.

"If you do attempt to test such a child, it happens in many cases that he gets an I.Q. which has no relationship to the degree of intelligence he subsequently reveals in his lessons.

"The shock he has received affects him, and often you notice that in the course of treatment his I.Q. appears to become greater as the treatment proceeds. This doesn't of course mean that his real I.Q. has altered. It simply reveals that our tests have failed."

He told me that in some cases the children do not seem to have any intelligent response at all, in our terms of judging intellect. "For psychological treatment there must be a certain ability on the patient's part to understand the methods of the treatment."

In short, psychology and psycho-analysis are, in the West, to some extent an elaborate kind of game according to rules of which the doctor is fully conscious and the patient partly so, and becomes progressively more so. The psycho-analysed patient becomes an adept at psychological terms and attitudes.

The patient understands the meanings of the pieces, and the moves in the game. But the Eastern child is sometimes simply incapable of playing such a game at all, because it is so utterly removed from his mental pattern.

"Sometimes, for example, a child comes along who refuses to speak. Then I have to help him to build a bridge between us. I ask him, for instance, whether he gets letters from home, or how he feels at home. Then usually he is able to speak—though often about something quite different. Our aim is to get the child to express his demands."

He quoted the example of a 10-year-old from Turkey who had been under treatment at the Institution. The child's educator had the problem of getting the boy out of the habit of saying "I can't," and "I don't know," whenever he was asked a question. After two or three months of treatment, the child was much better, but all the same, observed Dr. Dux with a sigh: "We noticed a certain poverty of impressions. He had very few words, and he found it difficult to talk about himself."

In fact, the professional psychologists, and still more the unprofessional, amateurish educators in the settlements, feel most of the time that they are up against a blank wall with the Oriental children.

The tests don't work. The child doesn't respond to the psychologist's elaborated game of concepts and symbols. Yet an utter lack of response, which would be certifiable with the Western child, means something different with the Oriental one. The possibility—particularly disturbing to the old-established Palestinian Jews—exists that the Oriental Jews and the Western ones have nothing in common. Even their religion and their conception of the meaning of the word "Jew" are completely different.

"These drawings," said Dr. Dux, showing me the work of some of the Oriental children, "are terribly primitive. Understandable enough, of course. Two houses on a sea coast, one of which resembles a human face. A wild and stormy sea with a ship on it, going towards another bit of coast, crowded with buildings. The two houses are the home that the child has left smiling houses. The ship is the ship that brought the child to Israel. There is a sea of hectic scribblings. The home the child has left and the place he arrives at, do not connect." It is quite clear, and yet somehow the primitiveness of such an obvious message has something opaque and therefore baffling about it. Here I am going beyond his own words, to read into them what I think he felt. "Such drawing is very primitive and very limited in the symbols available to the child, with which he can express himself."

Changing the subject, I asked him whether the hunger which certain children have endured, may not have produced neuroses different from those produced by the suppression of the sexual instinct, hunger being a different but even more basic instinct. Was there a special kind of hunger neurosis?

He nodded, and said:

"We had some Polish children nine years ago who made the journey from Poland through Russia, until they finally got, after terrible adventures, to Teheran, whence they were brought to Israel.

"These children ate an enormous amount at every meal. After they had eaten all they could possibly manage to consume, they would take the bread from the table and hide it in their rooms, in and under their beds.

"On one occasion, when we tried to tidy the room of one of these children, he began to cry. 'Why are you crying?' I asked. 'Because you've taken *my* bread.'—*My* bread, he said—I protested: 'You can't eat that. It's stale, and mouldy.' He answered: 'You've no idea what bread we used to eat. We ate bread which was months old, years old.'

"After this, I told my staff that whenever these children came to them saying they were hungry, they should give them food to eat at once. In many cases, when a child has eaten as much as he could possibly manage, an hour later he would ask to eat again. When he could eat no more, yet still seemed impelled to force himself to eat, we would say: 'Well, take the rest to your room.' When they knew that they could always do this, they were released from the compulsion always to want bread. Once one of them said to me: 'I've often stolen ration books from dead people in Siberia, and in that way I've sometimes been able to get more bread.' "

I went next to an Institution, called the Lasker Mental Hygiene and Child Guidance Centre of Hadassah, to talk there with the psychiatric director, Dr. Gerald Kaplan, who comes from England. I attended a conference of his staff in which a field worker was reporting on the problems of a mother in a Kibbutz whose four-year-old child suffered so uncontrollably from wetting, that she could not attend school. I forget the details of this case, except that I was struck by one of the questions Dr. Kaplan put to her. She had been saying that the mother appeared to have a good relationship with the child. To illustrate this, she recalled how pleased the mother had been at the way the child came forward to greet her on her arrival. "When the child did this, was the mother looking at you, or at the child?" asked Kaplan. The field worker thought a moment then said: "I don't remember." "Never mind," said Kaplan, "but it's always useful to note whether a mother takes the credit for herself or gives it to the child, when the child behaves nicely."

After the conference had finished, I was alone with Kaplan. He is my idea of what the English think to be "a good Jew." Intelligent, humorous, extremely reasonable and attentive to what others are saying, rather dapper, he seemed to characterize qualities of detachment which are the occasional results of Jews being "strangers." Even in Israel, his detachment made him something of a stranger, I thought, and I can imagine that he was suspected of being too English in his objective reporting of the situation in the Children's Institutions.

Like everyone else I interviewed in Israel, he gave me un-grudgingly of his time, and was a master of clear and lucid exposition.

To my first question, Kaplan said he thought there was no fundamental difference between the Eastern and the Western children. This reply, which rather surprised me, was the same as I had received from someone very different: Rabbi Rosenthal, co-worker with Youth Aliyah for the "religious children," a man of sparkling intelligence very different from the usual idea of the "orthodox" Jewish religionist. Rabbi Rosenthal's argument was that the children of East and West were fundamentally the same human beings, and that the bridge which could cross the gulfs between their Eastern and Western points of view was to be found in their religion. So the religious and the psychologist agreed that differences of background and en· vironment are only glaringly different colours imposed on outlines that are the same human personality in all men.

Dr. Kaplan went on to say that the problem for the immi-grant children is that they enter a new environment. The nearer this is to the one from which they come, the easier for them. Israel is still "Western" in most of its ideas and influences. So the Western child finds adaptation easy, the Eastern child extremely difficult.

The "Eastern" or "Oriental" child as such, he went on, does not exist. At any rate a child from Morocco may differ as much from a Tunisian child, as from an European one.

What is, however, common to the children from the Eastern countries is their so-called "primitiveness," different as are the forms which this may take. In general, this primitiveness means slowness in abstract thinking and a tendency to think in very concrete terms. Abstract thinking appears to be "magical" to the Eastern child. Thus he regards the fact that an effect follows its cause as being the result of magic. The educators, all of them Westerners, are brought up against children who cannot understand logical arguments or generalizations.

So it happens quite often that these children seem mentally defective from the point of view of the Westerner, when in fact they aren't.

Apart from this, the clues of behaviour whereby we judge whether children are normal, are different in the East, and the kinds of behaviour which with us would indicate disorders, don't necessarily do so with them.

For example, a boy of 11 or 12 who, when he is faced by a problem he cannot do, becomes violently hysterical, seems to us to be mentally disturbed. But with a Yemenite child this would be a normal reaction.

In the same way, if a 14-year-old girl suddenly develops blindness or paralysis for no organic reason, in the West we would think this an indication of organic disturbance. With a Moroccan girl, it would show that she was a little hysterical, but would have far less significance, and would not fit into a whole picture of her as an hysteric.

In the Kibbutz at Gaza, there was an epidemic of hysteria among the girls. One became hysterical and then three or four more girls caught the hysteria from her.

In many of the settlements there have been incidents, of which the following is characteristic: one girl receiving a letter from home, starts weeping, and then the whole group follow suit, until they all continue weeping for several hours on end.

Dr. Kaplan told me that the symptoms of this kind among the Oriental children seemed so alarming to the teachers (the madrachim) in the Kibbutzim, that when these children first began to arrive, reports from the settlements indicated that 15 per cent. to 20 per cent. of the children were mentally disturbed. However, when the trained psychologists went to the settlements, and examined nearly 2,000 children, they found that only about 4 per cent. were seriously disturbed. All the same, this figure raised a serious problem of how to deal with such children.

"We couldn't do more than just diagnose most individual

cases," he said. "To treat them all was impossible. So we tried to treat the children indirectly by helping the educators with their problems with the children. In as many cases as possible, we avoided removing the children from the settlements. We weeded out those children who had such 'disturbing' rather than disturbed qualities that they couldn't remain with the 'normal' children, and sent them to special institutions.

"In the end, we came to think of those difficult children, the 11 per cent. out of the 15 per cent. who had been complained of, and who now stayed on with their supposedly more normal companions, as 'disturbing' rather than 'disturbed' children.

"We tried to help the people in the normal environment to accept these children. We developed a system of staff consultations, and we sent advisers to the Kibbutzim to discuss with the educators *their* problems with the children.

"Each teacher—we found—is disturbed by a different type of child. We had to help the teacher to see the child not as a stereotype but as a human personality, basically the same as other human beings, but with his special problems.

"We learned to appreciate also the real significance of the non-application of our tests. What this revealed was that all these tests—to an extent we had never fully realized—were based on our own culture. The idea of an adult sitting in a room with a child and talking about the child's life and problems, is itself based on all sorts of assumptions and values. And these are upsetting to the Oriental child.

"The Oriental child's conceptions of time, ambitions, aims in life, and moral values, are all different from ours. Even the simplest performances based on a grasp of abstract ideas—such as for instance, arranging bricks in a familiar pattern—don't work with a child who has never thought of blocks in relation to other blocks in a pattern.

"When Yemenite children were presented with the simplest jigsaw patterns, they didn't know how to fit them together.

Such a child, seeing the parts of a puzzle, or even the completed thing, doesn't see a picture, for he cannot conceptualize it into what it represents. He just sees black or white or coloured blobs.

"Finally we tried to look for tests that did not appear to be culture-based; for example, letting them draw their own pictures in their own way, and trying to encourage them to express their fantasies. We have had to build up our own ideas of what is normal for these children."

In writing down my impressions of the ideas of the Israeli experts about the Oriental children, I am aware of contradictions. For example, it is rather difficult at a first glance to reconcile the marked differences Dr. Kaplan had noted between the Oriental and the Western children with his conviction that there is no basic difference. But here, I think the contradiction is more apparent than real. For it is in analysing the differences that a humanist like him, or for that matter a religious like Rabbi Rosenthal, discover the basic common humanity. Talking with the English psychologist and the orthodox Rabbi—both strikingly intelligent men—made me think that the only possible bridge between East and West is to be discovered either in an underlying common religious faith, or in understanding the separating effects of different environments on the fundamental human personality.

These conversations with experts lead farther than the problems of the children to the problem of East and West which overshadows the Jewish nation itself.

Meeting the psychologists and the educators in Israel sometimes you get—to a quite painful degree—the impression that the Westerners look upon themselves as superior beings who help the poor little Orientals to overcome the difficulties which have made them the problem children of the family of Israel. The Westerners assume the rôle of enlightened and conscious moral critics, the Orientals that of passive, undeveloped, un-self-conscious material waiting to be criticized.

Yet the adults who have come from Tunisia, Persia, Morocco the Yemen, etc., and who live in the slum encampments of the ma'abara do not always accept this criticism. They even show signs occasionally of feeling critical of the Westerners. Sometimes they fail to distinguish the European Jews from the white exploiters—almost as bad in some ways as the Moslems—whom they have left in the countries they came from.

Even though perhaps they have no constructive ideas about the way in which to make the Ingathered nation become a planned socialist society, they feel sceptical about the attitudes of the Western Jews. To themselves they appear to be the real Jews who have come to Israel for reasons expressed in their religion. Having arrived, they find that the Westernized Jews who are in control are often without religious beliefs. Moreover physically these Westerners appear to them to be simply Europeans, in exactly the same way as physically, to Western eyes, the Oriental Jew looks remarkably like an Arab. The aggressiveness, withdrawal into themselves, depression, lack of a sense of reality, reversion to a childish mentality, and other neurotic symptoms which the psycho-analysing Western Jews have noted in the ma'abara are undoubtedly the negative and self-destructive forms which this criticism of the home into which they have been ingathered, takes.

Every tragic situation contains the material of an excellent farce. Sometimes I think that the Ingathering of the Jews in this part of the world in this century under such tragic circumstances, and often with such tragic results, has also exceedingly funny aspects. That Jews find it so hard to accept other Jews as Jews is surely one of the most curious aspects of Israel. In the course of describing my impressions I shall come on other things, which strike me as amusing: for instance, certain aspects of the relationship between Israelis and American Jews. I hope, nevertheless, that the reader will not interpret my sense of the farcical within a situation where there is so much unhappiness following on such real suffering, as showing a lack of sympathy.

Later I went to the Villa Rosemarie, a home for chronically ill children with various physical ailments. It is a pleasant villa with a garden and with light, airy rooms in which conditions are made as pleasant as possible for the children in their circumstances.

All these children are suffering from severe illnesses: heart complaints, tuberculosis, rheumatic fevers, and so on. Many will be ill for the rest of their lives. Everything possible is done to enable them to work and lead a normal life.

These poor children, with their long thin limbs, their pigeon chests, their crouching stances, their over-bright eyes, are a pathetic sight. One boy had a swelling like an exposed sore extending from underneath his chin to the base of his nostrils, with his mouth like a split within this enormous swelling. There was a very thin, feeble boy with a bad heart disease, whom I saw sitting at his table studying a variorum edition of *Madame Bovary*. There was a charming little Yemenite child, looking like a golliwog, whom the others treated as a pet.

Dr. Cohen, in charge of these children, who showed me round, explained to me that most of them, suffering as they do from chronic conditions, not being bed-ridden, and coming from countries where illnesses like theirs are simply ignored, cannot understand that they are ill. That they should be told—when there is a drop in the temperature though the sun may be shining, to put on a jacket or a woolly garment, seems to them an unreasonable cruelty. One of them occasionally completes his recovery and leaves the home. Then it is difficult to make the others understand why he should go, and they stay behind.

In one of their rooms was one of those pathetic exhibitions of little things made from pathetically inadequate materials, which I saw so often in Israel.

I lunched with these children, and it was comforting that this was the best meal I had since my arrival. Afterwards I watched them playing in their garden, and it was clear that every effort was made to make them as happy as possible.

CHAPTER V

PEOPLE, CONVERSATIONS AND PLACES

O<small>NE</small> day Mrs. Y—— invited me to accompany her and Doctor W—— on his rounds to patients in the country.

We went first to a Moshav called Beith Zeit. A Moshav—Mrs. Y—— explained to me as we travelled in the doctor's jeep—is a co-operative settlement of people living in the country in small houses, who buy and sell their produce collectively. It is something half-way between an ordinary village of the Western variety, and a Kibbutz where no one has any money or (in principle) owns any property.

Beith Zeit has approximately 40 Egyptian and 40 Jugoslavian families. Amongst the Jugoslavs—Dr. W—— explained—there are many mixed Christian-Jewish couples in which husband or wife is Christian.

It is on a little plateau covered with olive and fruit trees, among the terraced hills. From the village I could see on one side Ein Karem, and on the other side the Swiss village. Looking down the valley below Ein Karem was a ruined Arab village: a place which had fitted into the landscape like teeth into a bone, was now torn up by the roots.

Beith Zeit itself consisted of a few small whitish houses, discreetly separate from one another, and not distinguished in any way. Each had its little plot of garden, and this and the trees give it a certain charm.

The people here keep chickens, and cultivate strawberries and other fruit. Dr. W—— observed quietly that he thought most of their produce went on to the Black Market.

We talked to an "oldest inhabitant" who showed us his house to which he had made a good many alterations, extending the inside and uglifying the outside. He said that within reason the community allowed the members to do what they liked in the way of managing their houses and bits of land. The village, he said, had five officers elected by the whole community, who did the administrative work. In fact, it was governed by an elected committee.

At this point, Mrs. Y—— asked me how I liked the village. Looking out over the landscape, I said I thought it was very nice. "Well," she declared, "I am appalled. I think it's dreadful." I took another look round me, and said tentatively: "Well, since you say so, perhaps it is rather." "I don't believe you ever say what you think, Mr. Spender," she declared.

I pondered the truth of this remark. It was true I had acted to her rather like Polonius humouring Hamlet about the cloud backed like a whale. It seemed to me though that Shakespeare is rather unfair to Polonius in satirizing him on this occasion. For a cloud is a very vague sort of shape often and if someone suggests to you that it looks like a camel at a certain moment, when you may have been thinking of something else, you are very likely to agree. A moment later, giving the matter more serious attention, you may well agree that it looks like a whale. In any case it may have changed shape in the interval.

Still in her role of Hamlet, Mrs. Y—— said: "Sometimes I see things which upset me a great deal. There is more thumb-sucking and bed-wetting among the children in the Kibbutzim than in Brooklyn."

This was really rather a horrifying revelation, and I promised to look into the matter when I next visited a Children's settle-ment.

We got back into the jeep and drove to Castel, a ma'abara situated on the crests of two hills. It was an encampment of huts made of corrugated iron, terribly hot in the summer, I should think. The people living here were Kurds and Persians.

On the hill opposite the huts, new houses were being built into which, I was told, the population of the ma'abara would gradually be moved.

A meal was being prepared for the schoolchildren at the main kitchen of the settlement. It consisted of soup—with no meat or bones in it—noodles, a chopped-up salad, beans and bread. The administrator told me that they never got meat here, and very little fish.

Through the open door of one of the tin huts I caught a charming view of a Persian baby, sitting like a figure in a miniature, with her legs crossed, on a rug. She had an air of delicate, waxen refinement, which made her little coat of red cotton seem an embroidered garment of silk, and the dirty rug on which she sat, a magic carpet.

We went from Castel to the Crusaders' Church at Aba Gezer, with immensely thick walls and an interior that seemed hewn out of the solid stone. The church, which was restored in the last century by the French, is in the care of a Benedictine monk, a smiling, intelligent old man with a great sense of the dramatic in his manner of showing us round. "Permettez moi de vous présenter à . . ." he says with twinkling eyes and a slight bow as he shows you the various objects in his care: the clear spring of water under the crypt, around and above which the church is built, altars given by the Canadian, the French and the British governments, the autograph of Lord Allenby in the visitors' book. "Est-ce que vous êtes Sud-Americaine?" he suddenly demanded of Mrs. Y——. "Dommage," he said when she explained that she came from New York, "because if you had been South American, you would have had pleasure in meeting——" some South American trophy—I forget what.

He gave us each a glass of an excellent liqueur he makes, and as we went through the churchyard laid his hand on a stone placed upright by the side of a footpath, saying: "Now if you want to steal something, I implore you to take anything but this. Tell me why I attach so much value to this stone." None of us could do so, and he announced that it was a stone on which prehistoric men sharpened their axes—or was it that they tailored their pelts on its cutting edge?

In Jerusalem, I gave two lectures on English modern poetry at the Hebrew University. Both were packed, which showed the immense interest in modern literature in this city where foreign books by contemporaries are almost unobtainable.

The most interesting of my evenings was perhaps at the Hebrew University, where after my first lecture I went to a party of the professors of the Humanities. This was a gathering of some of the most enlightened men of their time, as in any great European or American university where the Faculty is international. Looking back on my meetings it seems to me that under their courtesy and friendliness, most of the professors were sad, though too courageous and intelligent to express their disappointment.

For the Hebrew University of all institutions in Israel has experienced most bitterly the birth pangs of the new State. Founded a quarter of a century ago as the embodiment of the ideals of Zionism which would raise them to the highest pitch of intelligence in Jerusalem, the University is to-day cut off from its buildings on Mount Scopus, which is in Arab hands. Once a fortnight a convoy is allowed through Arab territory to relieve the guards of the Jewish enclave which contains the greatest library in the Middle East. As President Weizmann puts it in his preface to *The Hebrew University of Jerusalem* 1925-1950: "The Institutions and laboratories, which were equipped with so much effort, cannot function, just as the beneficent work of the Hadassah Hospital on Mount Scopus, which brought healing to Jews, Moslems and Christians for so many years past, is now at a standstill. It is a cause of profound pain and regret that international opinion, as represented in the United Nations and elsewhere, has for so long acquiesced in this state of affairs."

The Hebrew University is not only the embodiment of the idea of creating a new generation of Jews, but like the Weizmann Institute, it is a great centre of learning in the Middle East. Its loss affects the whole of this part of the world. Moreover, as anyone who reads the speeches of the former Chancellor Judah L. Magnes will realize, it is or was a centre of conciliation, for a group of men around Magnes were the chief advocates of the idea of a nation in which Jews and Arabs might peacefully co-operate.

Dr. D. W. Senator, Vice-President of the University, S. Halkin, author of the excellent survey *Modern Hebrew Literature* and translator of Whitman into Hebrew, and two ex-compatriots, A. A. Mendilow, head of the English Department, and J. W. Lever, were among the most confidently idealist Israelis I met. But under their faith I could feel their awareness of the difficulties through which their country was going, their fearful appreciation of the problem of the implicit conflict between East and Western Jewry which confronts the young State, and their sadness at the struggles between orthodox and unorthodox, Leftists and extreme Leftists, nationalists and liberals, which cast their shadows over intellectual life.

One of the professors who had come from England said that I could not have much idea from my visit of the misery in which most people lived in Israel. But on a different occasion he said, with the pride which makes it difficult for an outsider to write about this country without fear that he may be giving offence, that he felt that no one who had been in the country a shorter time than he had—14 years—had the right to criticize it.

With the help of Halkin's excellent book, and through several conversations with A. A. Mandilow and Sholom J. Kahn, I was able to form some idea of the qualities of Hebrew poetry in its English and German translations. It tends towards the rhetorical, and employs an imagery which owes much to the

Bible. But in some of the poems I read—especially those of Halkin himself—I had the impression that there is also a Hebrew poetry with an accurate and controlled development of metaphor, and showing the influence of the French symbolists. The colour, stony quality, and feeling of living in a biblical yet apocalyptic world, is shown very well in these concluding lines of *Tale of an Ancient Jerusalemite* (from *The Days of King Yanai*) by Uni Zvi Greenberg, who, in this translation by Sholom J. Kahn, reads as though he were the most interesting of the younger poets:

What I'd never known, I suddenly knew:
There's a kind of tear that does not open—
the tear-of-tears, that is not like dew
on the lid of an eye . . .
Like the blood it is, that cannot cry
in droplets; wrath must its utterance be ;
and its taste like the taste of the salt of my sea.

Joyous then through me this verse did shout :
Happy is he who prepares such a tear
to bring the day of redemption about !

The stones about me did jubilate :
they sang of an ancient Jerusalemite
returning to his father's estate.

Since then there's a flame in the point of my pen:
it's my home, and my garment to clothe my skin.

Since then has been sung rebellion's wrath;
and praises of heroic duties;
the power of sovereign authority;
and Kingship's beauties.

Since then has been carolled praise of the smith,
who from Philistine days has not lost his skill;
turning tools of the fields into weapons of vengeance,
from morning to evening laboring still—

He has seen the nation's disaster and learned

from the bloodshed: A people is blessed
that turns ploughshares-to-swords-in-day-of-distress;
in its evening's dimness, for morning has yearned;
and, like sons of the Exodus, is prepared
when it meets the sea to enter in—

that people will, in its regions, win
to Kingship, and see their beauty bared.

Jerusalem is a frequent subject of inspiration in modern Hebrew poetry, and the review *Zion* published a collection of poems about the city, by Molko Locker, Yehuda Halevi, Yehuda Karni, Ari Ibn-Zahav and Yehudah Alharizi, many of them exalted and powerful.

The subject most often discussed at the various gatherings I went to, was the Jews themselves. This is not just because the Jews are deeply introspective (which of course they are), but because the existence of the Jewish State has given them a new attitude towards being Jews. It is as though being a Jew in the Diaspora were an illness which they felt they had now recovered from. Sometimes the sense of recovery may seem over-emphasized, and occasionally the suspicion crossed my mind that the cure, like the effects of certain drugs, may produce a new illness all on its own, with a special name.

All the same the proposition: "We were Jews and are now Israelis," is a true one, and has something miraculously beneficial, if also depressing about it, like the effect on Europeans of becoming United States citizens. The effect is total and overwhelming and an object of wonder to the person himself.

As I have pointed out, in many respects, for the European, to be an Israeli is to be the opposite of what has been meant by being a Jew. It is rebirth, reincarnation a kind of after-life after-death existence. So to talk about being a Jew in Israel calls to mind images of spirits talking about life when they have attained Paradise—a rather uncomfortable and austere paradise with nothing to eat but curds and whey in it to be sure—but I dare say that is what Heaven will be like. To talk about being an Israeli, is to talk about one's own metamorphosis. To have been born in Israel is a kind of pseudo-tough condition of blessedness, referred to as being a Sabra: the sabra being the cactus plant which produces a fruit with a prickly exterior and a glucose-tasting soft pulpy, faintly edible, inside.

Undoubtedly most Israelis who have left Europe—especially the young—feel different and look different from the Jews of Warsaw, Vienna and Berlin. They are rectangular, rather than curved or stooping, with square shoulders, open chests, and a coming-straight-at-you expression.

Among their orange groves, and in their fields cultivated with their own hands, the Jews have got out of the ghetto like birds out of a cage into an open place of singing groves. It is impossible not to rejoice with them.

In this change of the Russian, Polish and German Jews into a psychologically and biologically altered type, there is hope also that the Oriental Jews will merge their separate characteristics into those of the sweet-and-prickly Sabras. Yet this hope is tinged with deepest misgivings which existed with the later European immigrants even before the immigration from Asia and Africa. The uneasiness is expressed by the question put laughingly to immigrants from Germany: "*Kommen Sie aus Deutschland, oder aus Ueberzeugung?*" "Have you come out of Germany or out of conviction?"

The Eastern Jews had come out of a religious urge which was different from the conviction of the early settlers, practical-minded visionaries, Tolstoyans, refugees of the 1905 Russian Revolution, who wished to found a democratic communism based on small communities in Palestine. The Eastern Jews had sometimes escaped violent persecution, whereas the Western ones, until the Hitler regime, had often come in order to frustrate their own tendencies towards absorption into the countries they had left.

In escaping from absorption, many of these European Jews

may feel that they had escaped from an influence more pervasive and more destroying of their integrity even than the ghetto. They had cured themselves of the neurotic guilt of the absorbed Jew at still remaining a Jew in a gentile community.

This immensely complex shame at being a Jew can even become the shame of being ashamed. It leads to that endless process of self-analysis which is typical of Jewish writers as different as Kafka and Proust; the self-analysis of the Jew who secretly despises himself because he has been absorbed, and who therefore takes the side of his persecutors who have ceased to persecute him. It is the inbred weakness of the members of a very old and ultra-refined race, who feel that because they are aliens they have no breeding.

The quality of aristocracy in the sensitive cultivated absorbed Jew like Proust, is what makes him both admire and hate the aristocrats of the country where he lives. The great novel of Proust—who has often, perhaps with too much simplification, been labelled a snob—is characteristic of this attitude. On the one hand, he has a boundless admiration for the French aristocrats, because they are in a rooted sense authentic. His meditations on the nuances of nomenclature, emphasize the irrelevant details which are precisely what gives the aristocracy its solid worth, its gilt weight, just as to the connoisseur the unseen handiwork at the back of a carving, the chiselling of the interior of a casket or an altar-piece, the irrelevant detail, are precisely what distinguishes the old craftsmanship from the vulgar new usage. Antique integrity is shown in the generous willingness to carry out a purpose even when it is unnecessary, whereas vulgar utilitarianism only recognized necessity.

Yet, on the other hand, with his admiration of the external, most physical and material aspects of the nobility goes a terrible insight into its moral and spiritual defects. For this reason, Proust has been called a satirist on the aristocracy by those who defend him from the charge of snobbism. His attitude though, is really ambivalent: it is that of the "absorbed" Jew.

He admires, and would like to imitate, those objective-seeming racial characteristics of the French nobility which he lacks because he is a Jew. His intrinsically aristocratic feeling for life is therefore forced on to a purely spiritual plane, from which he both admires and condemns that which is really in flesh and blood, but not at all in spirit, the aristocracy.

The two attitudes of admiration and contempt are both genuine, and even justified, because, from his point of view, there is certainly something to admire and also something to condemn. Proust is neither deluded enough to be a snob, nor single-minded enough to be a satirist. He sees two aspects of his aristocratic characters, admiring one and despising the other. At the same time the contempt turns against himself, because although he has the aristocracy of spirit which enables him to perceive the spiritual baseness of a Charlus, the spirit of Proust is a subjective quality, whereas Charlus' name has the objective quality of his blood. It extends beyond himself and has a validity which reaches into the earth and into the past.

The absorbed Jews never quite escape from the shame of not being the people they are absorbed into. Hence their worship of what is intrinsic to the people amongst whom they are absorbed—country life, fox-hunting, the English public school, snobbish international society, purity and breeding. Transparent in their intelligence, seen through and seeing through, they adore the opaque, even when it is stupefying.

The Israelis have overnight shed all this complexity and acquired simplicity. Nothing is more disconcerting to the visitor to Israel than this lack of complex, highly intelligent Jews. Instead, one meets everywhere people who in their outlook resemble the Quakers more than any other group I can think of. The spotlight of shame which always lit up their souls has gone out when they left the Diaspora, and perhaps a certain spiritual aliveness has gone as well.

The Eastern Jews do not have the self-torturedness of the Westerners. Apart from their religion, their attitude towards

Israel is that of any other oppressed people towards the country they exchange for the one which they have left. They ask themselves if they are materially better off than they were where they came from. If they change, they will not change in the same way as the Westernized Jews have changed. In fact, it is doubtful whether they will change at all, and quite possible that they will merely have the effect of orientalizing Israel.

The Israelis ask: "What do you think of Israel?" 10 minutes after you have arrived; and it was with difficulty that I persuaded the people at the Radio station in Jerusalem that it would be more sensible to broadcast such impressions before my departure rather than upon my arrival.

Such questions reveal an anxiety to see problems as they appear to an outsider, natural in a country which very few are allowed to leave, and where few books come in from abroad.

The many unavoidable restrictions on outgoings and incomings produce a certain feeling of claustrophobia in Israel. Even the visitor experiences a vague malaise, a feeling that he will not get away, and having got away he has a resistance to going back.

A question they often ask in Israel is: "Do you think we shall be able to produce great literature and art?"

A disturbing question. All the paintings I saw were in a European tradition, painfully adapted to the Palestinian landscape.

Although there is a great hunger for art in Israel, there are very few public galleries, and there must be still fewer collectors who can afford to buy paintings. Attempts are made on the Kibbutzim to encourage local talent, but the results are not encouraging.

In the towns, amongst the intellectuals, I was conscious of a feeling of provincialism. An intelligentsia formerly very cosmopolitan and travelled is cut off from vitalizing contacts abroad.

The intellectuals who fare best are undoubtedly those who

have thrown themselves whole-heartedly into education in the schools and universities, the collective life of the Kibbutzim, and other such work which makes immense demands on them. Those who cling to the life of individual values are depressed.

I breakfasted one morning with Walter Clay Lowdermilk, the famous American working for Israel on behalf of the F.A.O., and author of a remarkable book, *Palestine, Land of Promise*.

Lowdermilk has the look of a farmer from the Mid-West, with something about him of the poet or prophet also: an American father of his people who combines vision with a sense of the tremendous reality of the land, like Robert Frost. He has long unkempt grey hair and a round sunburned face which seems all furrows of awareness, puckering over bright, almost hidden eyes. He smiles in a way which makes you think that he might strike a rock in a desert and bring forth water. He has a folksy way of talking, and created an atmosphere like a W. C. Fields comedy in the midst of Jerusalem, whilst his wife, whom he called "Mother," brought us coffee and cookies.

Lowdermilk declared—he declares, rather than "says"— that Israel had the three essential conditions required for improving the country: (1) Pressure of necessity; (2) Intelligent people capable of assessing this necessity; (3) The determination and the needs to carry out these plans.

None the less, he had to admit that many of the politicians thought simply in terms of ideas and theories, and not of the real potentialities and limitations of the situation.

He expounded his own philosophy. It was that man should relate himself to the physical environment of the earth on which he stood, and in that way spiritualize the world by making the best of this environment.

To Lowdermilk nature is a book whose history is written on it by soil which has washed down the sides of mountains, sand which has blown in from the sea and formed deserts of

sand-dunes, rivers which have silted up, gullies which have
sunk through fissures in the earth, and dust-bowls which have
eroded farm-lands.

When he spoke about a gully, it was in the tones of a judge
arraigning a criminal. I trembled for them as he listed the
harm that they have done. Some parts of the country have
been so ruined by gullies, he announced, showing me maps
of hill-sides cracked and barren, that all we can do is seal them
off, plant a few shrubs and leave them as sanctuaries for wild
animals.

Working on surveys which comprise an inventory of the
whole country, Lowdermilk has formed extensive plans, for
redeeming desert, terracing mountain-sides, planting forests,
and bringing water to areas where there is none. He believes
that much more of Israel can be irrigated than the most optimistic Jewish experts had estimated, and he has put forward a
plan for diverting the water of the Upper Jordan to the
Valley of Esdraelon, and the excess waters of the Yarkon to
fertilize the Negev desert in the Southern part of the country.

Unfortunately—as is the case with many factors which might
immensely improve the situation of Israel—the feasibility of
these plans depends largely on the co-operation of the Arabs.
It is easier to be optimistic about altering the physical landscape
than about political relations with the Arab countries.

In *Palestine, Land of Promise*, the photographs show how
the Jewish settlers have saved part of their country. In one
photograph, you see bare rocky hills outside Jerusalem, with
no vegetation on them at all, apart from a few cactus plants.
In the next, you see the same landscape 20 years after the
foundation of the suburb of Beth Hakerem in this barren place.
It is a park-like country of pine trees with gardens under them,
surrounding villas. Other photographs—of the Balfour Forest,
planted on an eroded area—and the sand dunes, above which
the flourishing city of Tel Aviv stands, illustrate the same
lesson: that it is possible to make the desert flourish.

Lowdermilk is a prophet who has come to Israel because this is a country which needs and believes in prophets. But, of course, what is true of Israel is true of other parts of the world. Deserts can be carpeted over with fields, mountains can be terraced and covered with vineyards, water can be brought to places as yet unwatered. But to do these things requires that people should fix their attention on such projects and not on political theories and nationalist hatreds.

Lowdermilk's ideas form a frequent topic of conversation in Israel. An even more frequent one is the war—their war. This forms a kind of ground bass which no one ever quite forgets, underneath all the other subjects of conversation.

A few days after my breakfast with Lowdermilk, I was invited to breakfast with Ben ——— and his family. He called for me at the King David's, and we walked through those strange streets of modern Jerusalem—all of the same stone, and occasionally interrupted by wide open spaces with no houses but bare land grown with a few olive trees.

When we had come to a very large bare space like a large bald patch, we turned right and started walking up-hill towards the residential area, disconnected from my part of the town, where Ben ——— lived. He explained to me that this was formerly an Arab quarter. During the war the Arabs fired from these buildings across this patch to the houses in the street below the hill. But in the very centre of the patch there is a large building several stories high, with windowless walls on each side—it evidently was intended to be one of several buildings which had never got built—and Ben ——— explains that although this building was in the direct line of Arab fire, some Jews continued to occupy it.

He himself had taken a part in all this fighting—and I could well imagine him doing so, for he was an immensely strong, virile and courageous-looking man.

Innumerable conversations were like this, not just in

Jerusalem but in every part of the country. The war was on top
of every one, and was intermittent like the streets of residentia
Jerusalem, occasionally being interrupted by armistices and
then resumed again.

Mrs. Ben —— was a Londoner, so I felt able to ask her how
the war in Jerusalem really compared with the bombing of
London. "Well, I was in London during the whole blitz, but
the shelling of Jerusalem was far worse," she said. I can quite
believe this. The shelling was continuous for days on end, and
one must have felt oneself a far larger target than when lost
within the immensity of London.

The war, although on a small scale, was very intense and
took place in small areas. It resulted in a miraculous victory
The State of Israel was literally baptized with fire, and the
little country, left by the British in a badly disorganized condition, and attacked immediately from all sides by five Arab
countries, managed to survive. It is one of the greatest achievements of modern history, explicable partly in terms of the
conviction of the Jews in the righteousness of their cause,
partly in the complete lack of adaptation to contemporary
warfare of the Arabs.

Mrs. Ben —— went on to compare Now—to-day, March
26th, 1952, it was—with Then—the fighting in Jerusalem.
"To tell you the truth," she says, in the London accent which
was so sympathetic to my ears, "I'm sick at heart, really sick
at heart I am. Since then it feels as though everyone in the
country's become a wangler or a cheat. The whole lot of 'em,
from Cabinet Ministers right down to the immigrants new
arrived in the ma'abara, are involved in the Black Market.
Something's gone out of the new State already. The spirit
isn't what it was."

She went on grumbling in the English manner, and then
produced the classic and perhaps correct, but almost too well-
fitting argument, which explains the Black Market, whether
in Israel or in Europe after the war. The people had considered

it a duty to cheat the governments they lived under, and now they couldn't get out of the habit. They couldn't realize, it seemed, that Mr. Ben Gurion was Their Own.

"Well," said Ben ——, "I have a business here which is largely exporting," and he went on to say how he couldn't get quarto size paper—but only foolscap—nor envelopes with which to write to his clients. Finally, in order to do his business which brought in foreign currency, he had had to buy this paper on the Black Market. "That is one reason why people cheat. The regulations are so complicated and the bureaucracy so inefficient, that you can't do business through official channels, or you'd do none at all."

He then quoted the example of a car which he had not bought previously out of respect for the law and which now would cost twice as much, by the time he had obtained the papers for it— if he waited till the last paper was signed. They argued a bit about whether he should wait until this unpropitious moment.

This argument revealed the circumstances in which people go to the Black Market. A rationing system which scarcely gives them rations, a bureaucracy which stifles business, to- gether with the habit of regarding governments as enemies anyway. The Black Market is doubtless very bad, but certain countries would just die if everyone put his neck in the narrow noose of official channels, and the desire for survival is stronger than that for legality with most people.

Some of the criticisms which I heard of conditions in Israel were made doubtless because people were afraid of my hearing only the good side of things.

Almost the first person I met in the grounds of the Drive-in Hotel near Tel-Aviv a few days later was the son of one of the leading publicists in Israel. He invited me to have a drink and then he delivered a warning:—

"Maybe what I'm saying isn't good from a propagandist point of view, but I don't think it's good either that you should be told only the best about everything.

"It seems as if the tremendous wave of enthusiasm of four years ago has exhausted itself now, and there's a wave of disappointment, of apathy even. The few thousand energetic and devoted people who always carried the burden, whether in the army or the Kibbutzim, seem now either to be exhausted or doing other things. There is a drift away from the Kibbutzim into the towns. The idealists of a few years ago are already members of a generation which is being superseded.

"For example, take the *Jerusalem Post*. A few years ago it was a great newspaper which represented the enlightened views of an intelligent, vocal and influential section of the country. Now it expresses the views of a minority writing in the language of a minority.

"The heroes of the war have disappeared or gone into fairly lucrative jobs. For example, the proprietor of this successful hotel for American tourists was formerly the most audacious smuggler-in of arms to help the Jewish cause, in the country.

"I'm worried about how things are going to look in twenty years' time. I'm all in favour of the Ingathering, but all the same I don't want to walk down the road in Jerusalem or Tel-Aviv and see it full of Orientals sipping their Turkish coffee and not doing a stroke, in a general atmosphere of misery to which we've all been dragged down, as in any other Levantine city."

At that he turned to me and asked the inevitable question: "What do you think about Israel?"

I wrote my stumbling reply in my Journal, but find it does not bear writing out again.

He was wrong, though, in thinking that I was told only the best about everything. A few days previously I had lunched with Mrs. Weizmann, the wise and charming wife of the President, at the Presidential Residence at Rehovoth. Mrs. Weizmann had said to Mrs. Michaelis who brought me: "Show him the worst, as well as the best of everything." I am not sure whether I saw much of the worst, but I had a general impression of what it was like.

CHAPTER VI

THE PHASES OF YOUTH ALIYAH

MRS. MICHAELIS, whose name came into the last paragraph of the preceding chapter, took charge of me during most of my stay in Israel. She was responsible for the public relations of Youth Aliyah; but she looked after me with a kindness and sympathy which made my relationship with her, her husband, and their little son, David, far more than a business one.

As soon as I arrived in Jerusalem, we had several conversations in which she explained to me much of the history and work of Youth Aliyah.

When Hitler came into power in 1933 some of the Kibbutzim declared that they were willing to take over many of the children of Jews who remained in Germany, and fulfil the role of parents to them in Palestine.

That they did so was the result of the inspiration of Recha Freier, the real founder of Youth Aliyah, who foresaw already in 1932 the necessity of getting the children out of Germany.

In order to put Recha Freier's idea into practice, it was necessary to persuade the German-Jewish parents that they must allow their children to be separated from them, and that they could have confidence in the organizers of the movement for taking them to Palestine, and in the foster-parents.

One of the furies that plagued this generation of unfortunate children, was the unwillingness of the parents, even after the seizure of power by Hitler, to believe that the Nazis would really carry out their threats against the Jews. In 1933 many of them went on thinking that Hitler would do something to show that the anti-Semitism of his movement had only been propaganda, or that he would be so afraid of liberal opinion throughout the world that he would do nothing seriously to molest the Jews.

It is easy to enter into the situation of these parents who found themselves unable to believe that the unthinkable horrors of the future would happen, however strongly they had been warned by the Nazis themselves.

There was though, an American woman of Hungarian descent who, although she was seventy years old at the time, inspired confidence. This was Henrietta Szold, certainly one of the most remarkable figures in the Zionist movement in this century.

Henrietta Szold had first travelled to Palestine in 1909, when she became very concerned with the lot of the Jewish children, ailing and ill-educated, whom she saw suffering from the results of the (then) Turkish rule. On her return to America, she got the Hadassah Women's Club, an organization of Jewish women, which she herself had founded, and of which she was president, to begin the medical work of the Hadassah Organization in Palestine.

She went to Palestine herself to organize the Hadassah Medical Unit, in 1920. In 1927, she was elected one of the three members of the Palestine Executive Committee of the World Zionist Organization. In 1931, after her seventieth birthday, she undertook the task of making a survey of social service work in Palestine. In 1934, she undertook the organization of Youth Aliyah.

The biography of Henrietta Szold, by Elmer Ehrlich Levinger, is of the adulatory nature which characterizes most Zionist literature of the kind, and makes it difficult to discover the real character of the person underneath the surface of the writing.

Nevertheless, one must not be put off by the excesses of Zionist fervour. Henrietta Szold was evidently a person of remarkable courage, single-mindedness and human warmth. She combined real scholarship with the ability to apply her bookish learning to the details of practical work; great organizing ability with strength of imagination; and an abstract grasp of principles with the ability to treat every person with whom she came in contact as a single human individual. She would have seemed a great Christian to Christians, just as to Jews she seemed a great Jewess.

Her biographer records that when she was a child she expressed the wish to grow up to be the mother of many children; and I suppose that a psychologist might say that Youth Aliyah was the fulfilment of that wish. Maternity, in this case, came late, but certainly Youth Aliyah somehow seems the crowning achievement of her very full life. Yet there was something too full and warm about her development for the idea that her work was a sublimation of some other potentiality, to apply exactly. She was one of those people who apparently find complete fulfilment in social work. What is more rare, is that this did not seem to arise out of, or to cause, any warping of her human personality.

The parents trusted their children to Henrietta Szold because they felt that they were dealing with someone big enough to form a highly efficient organization, and great enough to remain a person. Mrs. Michaelis told me that during the first years of Youth Aliyah—when about 250 children from Germany arrived each year—Miss Szold knew every one of these children by name, and had a grasp of his or her problems.

She made a point of not only meeting each ship-load of children which arrived in Palestine, but of spending the first few days of their life in their new home together with the children, talking to them, getting to know them.

She was not only dynamic and highly personal, she was also attractive. At the age of 80 she had the power to fascinate her co-worker Hans Beyth, a man forty years younger than herself, to such an extent that his devotion to her became a serious problem for his wife and family. Hans Beyth, who was killed in the Jewish-Arab fighting, was himself one of the organizers of Youth Aliyah, and in his death is a hero of the movement. One sees his photograph on the walls of the settlements, together with that of Miss Szold. His friend Josef Yashuvi, in an interesting essay on Hans Beyth, seems to think that he was drawn to this work largely as the result of the influence of Miss Szold, who transformed his personality from that of an easygoing, rich young man, a lover of sport and a collector of old coins, into a devoted worker for Youth Aliyah.

So long as Miss Szold was alive, the bickering between different political groups, and orthodox and agnostics, which is so much a feature of every activity among the Jews, became melted down within the trust and respect all parties felt for her. She even managed to exorcise for the time being the most deplorable of all the tendencies of the educationalists: the attempt to influence the minds of the children in the interests of party politics.

Mrs. Michaelis, who worked with her, tells me that at the age of 80, Miss Szold was a worker whose energy exhausted all those colleagues who tried to keep pace with her. She was vain of this, as of her dress and her evident popularity—even if she was often bored by the public attentions she received, which interfered with work.

In the early days, those who came to Youth Aliyah were the 14-16-year-old children who had already belonged to German Youth Movements, and whose ideal was to be pioneers. Their ambition, when they came to Israel was to be members of the Kibbutzim and to work on the land.

Mrs. Michaelis described to me how she herself went to Czechoslovakia and Poland in 1938 and 1939, in order to try to get children out of those countries. All this time she knew that the war might begin and she herself not be able to get away.

One of the most serious obstructions to saving the lives of

the children was the Mandatory Government which would only grant a limited number of certificates to them. "When I got to Europe, I found that we weren't able to take all the children whose parents were willing to let them go," she said. So the children were sent to training camps, in order that those who proved most suitable, might be selected for immigration.

The Mandatory Government also set up a further obstacle by insisting on seeing the accounting books of Youth Aliyah, on the ground that more children should not be let in than the Movement could pay for.

The character of Youth Aliyah has altered all the time. First there were the children who came *aus Ueberzeugung*; then those who fled from the threat of war; and thirdly, now there are the Orientals.

Moreover the number of immigrants has gone on increasing all the time. It has therefore been difficult to carry on the tradition of giving each child the individual attention the children received when Miss Szold knew them all by name.

The main task of the educators to-day is to persuade the Oriental children that agricultural work in Israel is not the forced labour of such work in the countries they have come from, but is the voluntary co-operation of the communal groups in the Kibbutzim. In the Kibbutzim the children are able to see the example of the lives of the adults around them.

Another basic difference between the "Western" and the "Oriental" children, is that the European boys and girls who fled from Hitler, came for the most part from a well-educated middle class background. For the greater part they had few roots in Jewish culture, but had been assimilated into their European backgrounds.

The children who came from the East were assimilated, on the other hand, into Arabic life, whilst being at the same time aware, from the first awakening of their consciousness, of being Jewish. And their attachment to the Jewish tradition was of a primitive kind.

As Mrs. Michaelis pointed out, Youth Aliyah is really of crucial importance in the implicit conflict between the East and the West in Israel. It offers the great hope that differences of attitude may be healed in the homes where the children from all countries are brought together.

I asked her whether the general effect of this might not be the Westernizing of the Eastern children at the expense of their own culture. She agreed that this was the case. She said that 70 per cent. of the children now arriving in Israel were the Orientals. So it is a matter of a minority with Western standards and with a clear vision of how Israel should be developed, trying to convert a majority with Arab views and attitudes.

I asked whether there was any colour prejudice among the Western children. "Not that I know of in the Children's Villages or on the Kibbutzim," she replied. "But at David's" —her son's—"school she had recently come across an example. The mother of a Yemenite child at this school told Mrs. Michaelis that one day her son came home crying because the other children had shouted at him: 'Dirty little dark child!' The Yeminite child had asked his mother: 'Why do all these children speak German, and why can't I?'"

Mrs. Michaelis was being too optimistic—I learned to think —when she said she thought that such an incident could not occur with Youth Aliyah. Later I learned from the educators in the Kibbutzim that one reason which the Oriental children gave for resenting work in the fields was that the exposure all day to the sun made them more black, they thought. At a village where there were Yemenite children an educator told me of a boy who came running out of the wash-house, his whole body and face covered in soap-suds, shouting: "Look! Now I'm white like you!"

Mrs. Michaelis mentioned that there had sometimes been serious "wars" in the children's homes between Orientals and Westerners. On one such occasion, a law court of all the

children was set up, with judge, jury, lawyers and witnesses.
In this way the conflicts were brought into the open.

In the course of my travels I was to find several cases such
as that of a group of Indians who told me they had experienced
more colour prejudice among white people in Israel than in
India.

Youth Aliyah is financed entirely by voluntary subscriptions,
coming from abroad, mostly from the great Hadassah organization in America. But very large contributions also come from
England, South America, Canada and Australia. It is necessary
to raise between three and four million pounds yearly. Children
in the institutions are far more expensive to support than those
in the Kibbutzim. The arrangement with the Kibbutzim is
that Youth Aliyah pays each month the expenses of the children. But she admitted to me that of recent months, Youth
Aliyah had often been badly behind with these payments. They
have to pay the Villages before the Kibbutzim as unless the
expenses of the Village settlements were met, they would have
to close down. Sometimes the salary of the Educators is badly
in arrears.

It was fairly simple to raise money when the children who
came to Palestine were victims of the Nazis. Many American
Jews had relations in Germany who were persecuted, and it
was easy even for those without such connections, to identify
themselves with the children from Europe.

But no Westerner identifies himself with the Eastern children. They come from mellahs and slums where Westerners
were scarcely aware of their existence; and when they do learn
of it, their reaction too often is simply one of horror. Yet they
have in many cases been rescued from conditions almost as
horrible as those of the Concentration Camps. They also know
starvation, suffer from terrible diseases and only one in ten
of these children has the chance to survive beyond his twelfth
year, in the conditions from which they have come.

CHAPTER VII

PORTRAIT OF A VISIONARY

I WENT to visit Recha Freier, the remarkable woman who first thought of Youth Aliyah.

What struck me at once was her quietness, a quality so positive that it seemed even to influence her surroundings.

She has a pale, withdrawn appearance which makes her the kind of person whom at a first glance might not seem remarkable. But there is something about her which would make you look her way again: a certain rigidity with which she holds herself, the concentrated expression of her eyes, and the wispy untidiness of her hair, catching the light like an aureole.

Throughout most of my interview she sat very upright in her chair, with hands folded in her lap, except when occasionally she raised one hand with upward-pointing finger, in an almost apostolic gesture.

She looked as a portrait might by Douanier Rousseau, if he had painted the most inspired-looking woman in his village and called his picture "The Saint."

The stone floor of her room was bare, and the furniture, except for a table and the chair on which she sat and my own chair opposite hers on the further side of the table, was ranged against the walls of the room. Between pieces of furniture, there were bookshelves with books in several languages.

Recha Freier's plain unpretentiousness, combined with her air of burning quietness, reminded me of Quakers I used to meet sometimes in the London flat of my grandmother, who was herself a Quaker.

There were pauses in our discussion, because she obviously had no small talk with which to fill up conversational gaps.

The interview therefore consisted of clumps of closely knit sentences when Recha Freier expressed her views, followed by silence when the subject had been disposed of.

We started off with a long silent pause. I then remarked that it was a lovely day. Mrs. Freier assented, and there was another silence. I asked her then whether this part of Jerusalem where she lived was on the outskirts of the city.

"No," she said, in a level, slightly monotonous voice. "This is a quarter which continues to extend a considerable distance before you reach the country. The road outside the window is the direct route from Jerusalem to Bethlehem. It is the road on which King David went when he left to fight against the Philistines. They say there are a great many ghosts here. It is true that often in the middle of the day there is an extraordinary wind."

She stopped on an almost-smile, her hands folded in her lap, waiting for me to start a new subject.

I said I had come to Israel in order to learn as much as I could in a few weeks about Youth Aliyah.

"Ah," she said, and sighed. Then she said: "Ah," again.

I said I had been told by Mrs. Michaelis that the idea for Youth Aliyah had originated with her.

"Yes. It was one of those ideas which come to me. I had no experience of social work but in 1932 several young boys I knew in Germany lost their jobs and all possibility of future employment, on account of their being Jews. So this idea came to me. At first no one would take it seriously. Even in Germany where the Jews were already being persecuted, they laughed at me. Even Miss Szold would have nothing to do with it at first. Not even Miss Szold."

She paused again. Then in a more vibrant voice, she went on: "Only the children themselves were on my side. Yes, the children understood the idea before their parents did. They wanted to go to Palestine."

She told me how she asked permission of the headmistress of a Jewish People's School in East Berlin to speak to her children about the reasons for going to Palestine. Permission was granted very unwillingly.

"The meeting took place in the presence of the headmistress," Mrs. Freier wrote, in a document which she gave me. "I inquired from the children concerning their plans after they left school. I told them about my scheme. The children discussed it excitedly and with enthusiasm, and I then knew that I could rely on those who formed the most important factor in the situation.

"Next day, they crowded into my room, waiting to put down their names."

After this, she had to get the support of the Jewish community, in order that she might obtain the means, and also the applications for Immigration Certificates, for the children. Miss Szold, together with most of the Jewish community, and many of the parents of the children concerned, remained sceptical. But the children were for her.

In June 1932, Dr. Siegfried Lehmann, the great pioneer of Youth Training in Palestine, who had himself brought a group of children out of Germany many years previously to the village of Ben Schemen, interviewed Mrs. Freier's candidates, and offered twelve of them places in the Children's Village at Ben Schemen.

After this, money was raised from private sources, and the first twelve children left Berlin. In Recha Freier's words: "The Anhalter Station trembled under my feet. The work was born. No one could ever prevent it. It would grow, and the young people who stood excitedly round us, would attain their goal. They themselves never doubted this. There was an air of jubilation as the train steamed out. The parents wept."

After the Nazi seizure of power in February 1933, Mrs.

Freier founded an organization to take care of the children of Jews in concentration camps.

Organizations called *Jüdische Jugendhilfe* and *Arbeitsgemeinschaft für Kinder und Jugend Aliyah* (a fund-raising body) were formed in Germany, with, in 1936 and 1937, groups in Poland and Czechoslovakia.

These organizations not only trained children and got them away from Germany, but they also performed useful rescue work in desperate situations. For example, in 1938, many Jews of Polish origin were driven out of Germany. Poland also refused to take them in and they were put into a No Man's Land between the Polish and the German borders. Many of the children of these unfortunate people were rescued and got away, eventually to reach Palestine.

When Germany invaded Poland, other children escaped into Lithuania and went by way of Russia to Palestine.

The night before Hitler entered Prague, Youth Aliyah removed a group of Jewish children from the city. And so always the organizers tried to get the children away before the Nazis came in.

In 1938 the *Jüdische Arbeitsgemeinschaft* office was moved from Germany to England. From then on the operations to get the children away from Hitler's clutches were directed by telephone from London.

At this time it became impossible to send the children to Palestine, because the Mandatory Government refused to grant Immigration Certificates. So it was decided to remove thousands of children out of Germany into neighbouring countries—Sweden, Denmark, Belgium, Holland and England. From these countries, the children were able to proceed gradually to Palestine, at first by way of France, and then, after Italy had entered the war, through Russia.

The Jews were extremely effective agitators in the cause of the children. For example, in 1938, the Danish Minister of Justice was reluctant to give permission to the Jewish children

to enter Denmark. Accordingly all the fire of Jewish agitation
was directed at him. It so happened that every week the Danish
Minister of Justice has to devote an hour to receiving any
pleaders coming to him with complaints. Every week someone
was sent to put to him the cause of the Jewish children. The
organizers of aid for the children inserted an advertisement into
the Danish newspapers asking for the names of those who were
willing to take a Jewish child into their own families. They received hundreds of answers. They then circularized the answer-
ers, asking all of them to send telegrams to the Minister of
Justice on the same day, announcing their wish to care for a
Jewish child. The result of this agitation was that 450 children
were admitted into Denmark.

Meanwhile Recha Freier formed another plan: to send
children to Greece, Turkey, Bulgaria and other countries
from which it was possible to transport them by ship to Palestine, and where they might wait until they obtained the
certificates.

Before this could be done, the war broke out. Many of the
children were then sent by the Nazis to Forced Labour Camps
where, with a large "J" painted on their knapsacks, they were
forced to do work which often broke their mental and physical
health. Many died in these camps.

In 1941, Recha Freier went to Jugoslavia, to inquire whether
there was some means of smuggling the children to Palestine.
From Jugoslavia, she sent helpers to Germany who conducted
the children across the frontier.

When they had got the children into Jugoslavia, they then
had to smuggle them into Palestine. Here help came from many
quarters—some of the unexpected. Amongst those who, at
this period helped, were the British Embassy and the Jugoslav
police.

The arrangement came to an abrupt end when some over-
zealous Jugoslav police arrested a group of Jewish emigrant
girls. The authorities treated these children very well during

their detention, but the incident caused an uproar in the Jugo-slav press when people realized the plight of these unfortunate Jewish children. Such publicity was bad for Germany at a moment when she was planning to occupy all Europe. After this the Nazis allowed no more Jewish children to leave the country.

In the rest of this chapter, I shall try to draw the picture of the story of Youth Aliyah in firmer lines, and to fill in a few details. I draw here very largely on Norman Bentwich's ex-cellent book, *Jewish Youth Comes Home*, published by Gollancz in 1944.

We have seen how Recha Freier had the idea for Youth Aliyah as early as 1932. It was comparatively simple for her to get the support of the Jewish Youth in Germany. The difficulty was to get the children who supported her so en-thusiastically into Palestine. The first Meshakim (or local councils) in Palestine to say that they would accept groups of children were Ain Harod, Geva and Dagania. Next the Zionist Organization in Germany were persuaded to provide the funds without which the children could not be sent. This could only be done when the members of the Jewish National Council in Palestine had been persuaded. Mrs. Freier went to Palestine to win their approval, in which she was successful. The next major problem was that of obtaining from the Administration certificates of immigration for the children. Fortunately in 1932, the newly appointed High Commissioner, Sir Arthur Wachope, was sympathetic to the needs of Jewish young people. Thus, as I have described, the first group of a dozen children were able to leave the Berlin Anhalter Bahnhof for the village of Ben Shemen.

After Hitler had become German Chancellor a great stimulus was given to the ideas of Youth Aliyah. In May 1933, Dr Chaim Arlosoroff came to Berlin. As one of the heads of the Jewish Labour Federation he proposed to the German Zionists that they should accept a plan for emigrating thousands of

G

young people, along the lines laid down by Recha Freier. But on his return to Palestine, Arlosoroff was murdered.

Now, when things were most discouraging, Miss Szold's support was at last fully enlisted.

That she supported the idea of Youth Aliyah, transformed the situation. Those who had been uneasy and unwilling now had confidence. She worked out a scheme whereby the young people should be given an initial training in Germany with the teacher (the Madrich) who would eventually accompany them to Palestine. When they got to Palestine, they would be attached to a community for two years. Mutual arrangements were made between the villages and the Movement. In return for board and education, the settlements would receive a small amount of money. After two years the group would be responsible for its own support, the idea being that, whether they founded a Kibbutz or went into one, they should remain together.

Miss Szold, at her advanced age, who was in Palestine, undertook the prodigious tasks involved in getting certificates out of the Mandatory Government, making arrangements with communities and finding quarters for the children to live in. Meanwhile groups of loyal friends of Youth Aliyah in Palestine devoted themselves to forming an organization which gradually won support in America and England.

Mr. Moshe Kol, the present head of Youth Aliyah, described Miss Szold to me as the greatest Zionist of the 20th Century. Her essential qualities were surely the combination of vision disciplined by scholarship with complete attention to the details of practice and administration; and of power of abstract thinking, with an almost perfect understanding of what was going on in the minds of the children. As Norman Bentwich excellently puts it: "As with Hadassah, so with Youth Aliyah, she made it not a party achievement, but a religion of good works. She exercised an influence over all the sections in the country and over communities rent with party factions. She could satisfy still the most profoundly religious pietists and the most liberal and 'godless' Socialists. She . . . was the one person in Palestine or outside Palestine who could unite the sections for a common task." He quotes a letter which reveals on the one hand her full realization of what was discouraging and even wrong about the present Palestinian Jewish generation, on the other her faith in the essential principle of Youth Aliyah, a principle which may still heal the internal dissensions of the Jewish State: "I may as well confess that life here does not make me happy. As was to have been expected, again there is a generation of the desert which will have to perish in order to fructify the soil. First a synthesis of the Jews gathering here from everywhere will have to be brought about, and then we may have to expect the life here to have some gracious aspects. And yet things are not so bad that you must insist upon my coming home . . ." This open-minded open-eyed attitude is surely very exceptional in a visionary and has real greatness.

The first group of Youth Aliyah coming to Ain Harod arrived in February 1934. But within a year of this date twice that number of certificates had been granted by the Administration and used by Youth Aliyah.

When Hitler came to power, many Jews had continued to believe that nothing very terrible could happen to them. But the purges, the anti-Jewish decrees, the Burning of the Books, and the Concentration Camps, made them realize by 1935 that perhaps the worst pogrom in history could take place in the Germany which sometimes claimed to be the most civilized country in the world, in the middle of the 20th Century. In August 1935 there was the Nuremberg Party Day when Hitler announced still worse measures against the Jews. Just after the Nuremberg Rally, the first Youth Aliyah Conference was held at Amsterdam. As a result of this meeting Miss Szold tried to obtain 350 certificates for immigrant children. The High Commissioner granted these, but before they could be utilized, there were the Arab-Jewish riots of 1936, which resulted in a reversal of the Administration policy. Hundreds of children waiting in Europe to escape from the Nazis, and being trained in the Youth Aliyah Camps, could not get away. The flow of children was all but stopped until the summer of 1937.

Nevertheless, Youth Aliyah was growing. Teachers were being trained and so were the children who arrived from Europe By the summer of 1937, 1,600 children had been brought to Palestine. But by now events were moving rapidly to a climax. In 1938 there was the invasion of Austria by Hitler, followed later in the year by the macabre agreement at Munich which led in turn to the fall of Czechoslovakia. The number of certificates issued increased but the number of victims of the Nazis grew at an even greater rate . . .

By 1938 the catastrophe of the Jews—shortly to be followed by that of the whole of Europe—had assumed almost unthinkable proportions. Jewish Communities did their utmost to meet the situation, but in this they were frustrated as much by the policy of the Mandatory Government in Palestine as by that of the European governments anxious for appeasement. The British Government was by now frightened that immigration would lead to its entering an anti-Fascist war, with the Arabs against them (the myth of the invincible Arab is amusingly dealt with in Koestler's *Promise and Fulfilment*). Diplomacy had reached the stage when the children could not be saved, for fear of annoying the Arabs. To quote Norman Bentwich again: "The Colonial Secretary stated in the House of Commons in December that they (the government) could not agree to the reception of the large number, though they did grant a substantial allocation of children's certificates."

In a very British way, however, we to some extent redeemed the disgrace of our public behaviour by the decency of our actions as individuals. England found homes "for close on 10,000 children from Germany, Austria and Czechoslovakia," between December 1938, and the outbreak of war in September 1939. "It is noteworthy" (Bentwich goes on) "that the total rescued in England in nine months was equal to the total rescued in Palestine in nine years. Four-fifths of the whole were Jewish boys and girls."

I have already indicated the state of affairs at the beginning of the war. Bentwich describes how during the Zionist Congress held in Geneva in August 1939, the news of the Soviet-German pact broke. The representatives of Youth Aliyah organizations left the Congress and went to their various countries to make, if possible, arrangements to save thousands of children in imminent danger of being shut into the barbed wire encampments of occupied Europe.

In the last few days before war, some children were got to Holland, some to Denmark and Sweden, and a few to England. A group embarked from Italy, and after many adventures following on the declaration of war, reached Palestine. Others, with immense difficulty, managed to trickle out of Eastern Europe by devious routes. Altogether, throughout the war years, a thousand children each year got to Palestine.

Even after the outbreak of war, the children stood a good chance of being victimized by the immigration policy of the Mandatory Government, blowing hot and cold, sometimes issuing certificates, sometimes withholding them, even if they escaped the terrors of the Nazis. The terrible dramas of the ships which, having escaped from occupied Europe loaded with immigrants, were not allowed to land, showed this. On the *Struma*, which sank in March 1941, fifty children of its 750 passengers were intended for Youth Aliyah. The *Darien* sailed for five months up and down the seas before it was allowed into Haifa. On board it there were sixty children. Miss Szold obtained permission from the High Commissioner for Youth Aliyah to adopt them. Youth Aliyah also adopted the Bulgarian children rescued from the *Salvador*, lost in the Sea of Marmora.

This period of the history of the Jewish children resembles

that terrible year—also connected with Jerusalem—of the Children's Crusade, when the children were purely victims of the violence and folly of an older generation in a century which we of the present one regard as scarcely civilized. The most terrible experience was that of the so-called "Teheran" children — 856 Polish children arriving in the autumn of 1942 at Dahlevi on the Caspian Sea. These were the children of 14,000 people—Christians as well as Jews—who had escaped from Poland at the time of that country's invasion in the first weeks of the war.

Norman Bentwich quotes Miss Szold's report on these children who had trailed their way through the Ukraine, Siberia, and Turkestan. "They had been sleeping in the woods, half-naked, exposed to disease, eaten by vermin, starved— guiltless. The Jewish communities through which they passed took them in and cared for them to the best of their ability."

Youth Aliyah undertook to adopt these children who pro- vided problems as difficult and different from those of the earlier immigrants, as the "Oriental" children in time were to prove different and difficult.

So after the early phase of getting the victims away from their persecutors before the persecution had started, there followed the second war-time phase of rescuing escapees from the Labour Camps and the Gas Chambers. Then at the end of the war there followed a third phase, lasting from 1945-1948, of rescuing the survivors of the war. Polish children who had been sent back from Russia to Poland, subsequently spending long periods in U.N.R.R.A. camps in Germany and Austria, had left secretly for Palestine. En route they were often arrested by the British and sent to camps in Cyprus. During this phase most of the children looked after by Youth Aliyah were from the Balkans. Many of them had been schooled first in the Nazi Concentration camps and then in the camps at Cyprus for illegal immigrants. Many of these children had lost one or both parents.

The fourth phase—the one I encountered—began in 1948 with the creation of the state of Israel. The last children rescued from Europe had now arrived. But the creation of the Jewish state, followed by the Jewish-Arab war, was a sign for persecution of Jewish communities in the Arab countries. So the kind of immigration I discuss frequently here began—from North Africa, Tripoli, Yemen, Persia and Iraq. Other Jews from all over the East, flowed in because they thought the Biblical prophecies of the Ingathering had been fulfilled.

This book is not intended as a history of Youth Aliyah; and the sketchy account I have given in these pages is meant simply as a background to my cursory travel impressions. It will, I hope, lead those readers who are interested, to read Norman Bentwich's *Jewish Youth Comes Home*, from which I have taken most of this information. I hope too that I have given the reader some idea of the waves of circumstances which produced the waves of immigration—different in character in each five years. I hope that he will feel interested enough to look further into the personality of Henrietta Szold, surely one of the few saintly figures the 20th Century has seen. I hope that in his mind there will be a picture of the children leaving the places where they have been victimized, and going in ships to the country promised to them as their national home, where they are received by Henrietta Szold or Hans Beyth, her adjutant. In his mind the reader should be able to visualize them going to the sorting-out centre near Haifa, from which they are distributed to one of the several hundred settlements and Children's Villages, whose institutions await them. He should see a *madrichim* attached to each group of 20 or 30 children, and in addition to this a system of house mothers and leaders chosen from among the children themselves. He should imagine the children learning Hebrew—their common language—and dividing the rest of their studies equally between ordinary schooling and agricultural training. Most of them will go onto agricultural settlements in the Kibbutzim or

Kvuzoth. Those who show aptitude for other things than agriculture will receive special vocational training.

In 1945, Henrietta Szold died. Two years later her closest collaborator, Hans Beyth, was killed during the war. The present head of Youth Aliyah is Mr. Moshe Kol, who is also a member of the Executive of the Jewish Agency and a leading member of the Progressive Party of the General Zionist Movement. I met him several times in Israel, and could see that his personality combined the qualities of intelligence and humanity which are in the tradition of Henrietta Szold.

England and the British Dominions contribute very largely to Youth Aliyah, which has a budget of about I£4,000,000 yearly. However, the greatest contribution comes from Hadassah, the Women's Zionist Organization of America. Hadassah is such a remarkable achievement that an account of Youth Aliyah would be incomplete without a few words about it.

Hadassah was founded in 1912 by a group of 14 women, with the aim of sending two trained nurses to Jerusalem to teach mothers how to care for their babies and to combat the dreadful eye-disease, trachoma. Out of this initiative—thanks very largely to Henrietta Szold—there grew to-day's tremendous organization which has cared for the health and education of the Jews in Palestine. Hadassah—although Zionist—is a monument to the principle of American generosity, which is based on the profound conviction of many Americans that they should share their material advantages with peoples in less fortunate circumstances. This feeling, when appealed to in a responsible way, has resulted in a tremendous flow of gifts from America to Europe of recent years. It is a national feeling related perhaps to the feeling of individual Americans that part of them still belongs to a family abroad to whom they are bound by human ties. With the American Jew this feeling is twice as strong as with non-Jewish Americans, as a document issued by Hadassah during the war against Hitler, and putting to American Women Zionists reasons why they should belong to Hadassah, makes clear. "I belong to Hadassah because I am an American bred in the conception of 'liberty and justice for all.' I cannot say to my fellow Jews across the ocean: 'I am free. You shift for yourselves'," is stated in this manifesto. Here also are the aims of Hadassah:

"I want to increase Hadassah's Health Services so that the people of Palestine to-day and those who will come from Europe tomorrow shall be strengthened for their pioneer labours. I want Hadassah's child care and feeding projects and its vocational training programme to reach more children, to keep them sturdy and well and to teach them, useful skills. I want to enable Hadassah, through Youth Aliyah, to rescue more Jewish children and settle them in Palestine, where loving kindness, proper care and freedom from fear will erase the memory of the brutality they have known. I want Hadassah to help the Jewish National Fund extend the national land holdings . . ."

In short the aims of Hadassah are nothing less than to support the health, education and construction of another country—except, of course, that to American Zionists Israel is their own country. Even so, it is voluntary taxation on an immense and unprecedented scale. Nor do the Hadassah ladies (and their husbands) limit their effort to sending money. They take an almost overwhelming interest in the results of their generosity. Unending aeroplane-loads of Hadassah ladies arrive in Israel, travelling around the country, taking notes and making criticisms.

This great generosity has its less sympathetic and even ludicrous aspects, of which I give one or two examples in these pages. It would be easy for a Christian observer to comment that charitable Jews blow their own trumpets too much. But the Jew might retort that Christians are so afraid of having the wrong motives for their charity, that they often stop being charitable altogether, or limit their acts to generous feelings untainted by the odour of money.

Hadassah has now about 300,000 members, with officers and boards functioning in 19 regions. There are 800 chapters, groups and professional divisions. These chapters are sometimes so large that they have to be broken up into smaller groups.

Its activities can be stated simply as the dual ones of raising money in America and spending it in Israel. Its primary work in Palestine has been care of health. Between 1918 and 1951 over 2,000,000 people attended Hadassah clinics and over 300,000 patients had been treated in Hadassah hospitals. At Mount Scopus in Jerusalem (now in Araba territory) there is the Rothschild-Hadassah-University Hospital, one of the greatest medical centres in the world, with 21 departments. This is only the best known of the achievements of Hadassah, which has been instrumental in achieving a remarkable decrease in infant mortality in Palestine.

Hadassah has also promoted vocational education in Israel, for clerical work; dressmaking and tailoring; and cooking, for girls: carpentry; metal work; leather work and other manual work for boys. But the greatest work among the young Jews has been Hadassah's help for Youth Aliyah, for which it has been the chief sponsor in America.

In 40 years Hadassah has grown from being a small organization for training a few nurses, into a main channel for transfusing life-blood into a young nation. It is difficult to think of any parallel charitable organization in the world to-day.

CHAPTER VIII

MAPAM KIBBUTZ

DURING the last week in March the fields burst into flower
—masses of yellow daisies, and red poppies like bright
shreds of torn, crumpled paper, among steel-green grass that
swayed stiffly and gleamed in the white sun. Phlox, tulips,
cyclamen, gladioli, irises, asphodel, rock roses—these were
only a few of the flowers whose names I knew, amongst so many
which carpeted whole mountain sides. The reddish rocks sur-
mounting the hills of the Carmel range rose like towers and
castle walls above the masses of blossom.

The fields and the orange groves, with their sweetly-piercing
scent, seemed ten times more fertile than they had done ten
days previously when I arrived in Israel.

The first of the Kibbutzim where there was a Youth Aliyah
group which I visited, was Netzer Buchenwald, so called
because the original founders of it had come from Buchenwald.

Netzer is a charming place, an old German Templar settlement, with three-storeyed, wooden, verandahed buildings of a
colonial-style architecture. It is enshadowed by eucalyptus and
many other trees cool and green against the yellow-ochre walls
of the buildings which are a bit worn and tumbled-down. The
whole place has a relaxed air, unlike most of the Kibbutzim.
It is surrounded by the farmlands of which the Kibbutz is
the hub.

In the reception room where we waited for some minutes for
the "educator," I noticed a large photograph album, to which
was attached a section of thick and tough barbed wire. It con-

tained relics of Buchenwald—a few faded photographs of prisoners there, some specimens of money which were in circulation only within the concentration camp, and so on. The thing was very haphazard and incomplete and made the same impression as the camp.

The educator was a man—a Bulgarian, I think—of sensitive, but firm appearance with a mass of untidy black hair and features at once strong and soft, like those of a violinist or a sculptor.

He told me that when he came here he didn't know whether to ask Youth Aliyah to send children from one, or two or several countries. He decided that if all the children came from the same country they would talk the language of that place together, and not learn Hebrew. If they came from two countries they would tend to divide into two groups.

So in the end he thought it best to mix together as many different nationalities as possible, so that the children would perforce communicate through their one common Israeli tongue—Hebrew. He has children from sixteen different countries, with only two or three from each country.

The children chatter away together in Hebrew—their common tongue. After they had been there only a short time, he noticed that friendships were almost always formed between children coming from different countries.

"Look," he said, pointing down from the verandah where we were standing to a group of children playing ball in the garden below: "Bulgarian, Turk, Egyptian, Roumanian, Belgian, Iraquian, Moroccan, another Bulgarian, Polish, Persian, German . . ."

They certainly looked like relations coming from one family with a varied background—cousins born of mixed marriages, perhaps. "The difficulty we experience," he went on, "is that the children who come from those countries where there is no heritage of learning acquired from their parents, do learn less easily than the others. The children themselves, though, are not conscious of these differences. For them there is soon only one country which they come from, Israel."

The atmosphere of this place was delightfully easy. Perhaps too easy, but I found it sympathetic. Afterwards, Mrs. Michaelis said that she thought I would notice its difference from other places. She thought that perhaps the reaction of the inhabitants from Buchenwald had led to their not wanting to take too much trouble about the appearances of their surroundings. Perhaps they just wanted to be easy-going. At any rate, the tension which I usually noticed in Israel seemed absent here.

The children though, seemed to benefit from this. I never noticed such a happy-seeming family, as they all gathered round a puppy from the farm, which a small Egyptian was holding in his arms. An older child was receiving instructions from a farm labourer as to exactly what bit of land on the farm he was to take his team to that afternoon. He was studying the place on the map, with a look of responsible concentration on his face.

I ate with these children. The meal consisted of what I mentally called a "mess of pottage", one of those bowls of something between a cheese and a meatless stew, with which I got familiar in Israel. There was also a minute fish, like a freshly-fried sardine. But it was a real fish, with fins and back-bone and a tail, and for that reason delightful. It was not the usual anonymous slice of something simply called fish, sent I dare say from social democratic England to social democratic Israel.

Nothing could have been more different from Netzer-Buchen-wald than the atmosphere of Negbah-Kibbutz, the next place we went to. Negbah is a Kibbutz with a Youth Aliyah children's settlement about five hundred yards distant. It is run by the extreme left-wing party, Mapam. Some weeks previously, a group of supporters of the moderate socialist party, Mapai—followers of Ben Gurion, the Prime Minister—had left Negbah and joined another Kibbutz, finding it impossible to endure

any longer the atmosphere of purist extremism which characterizes this place.

Such secessions in the Kibbutzim of whichever socialist
group happens to be in the minority, have been a feature of
life in the Collective Settlements lately, as the result of the
extremely bitter divisions of the Left.

Negbah Kibbutz was entirely destroyed during the war, and
the buildings of the settlement are all new. On the great plain
looking down to the sea across a fertile landscape gleaming with
new projects, the incline where Negbah is situated is dominated
by the British-built concrete police-station fortress—one of
fifty erected at strategic points all over Palestine by the Mandatory Government—about a mile above Negbah. During the
war this was occupied by the Arabs who utterly destroyed
Negbah, killing many people.

Mrs. Michaelis had brought with her some sign-boards to
fix on the various school buildings of the settlement. They
indicated that such and such buildings had been put up by
such or such a Chapter of Hadassah, the American Zionist
Women's Organization whose immense works of charity are
responsible for so many of the achievements of Youth Aliyah—
and indeed of Israel. During our drive to Negbah she had told
me, with much humour, that she was nervous about bringing
the plaques: on a previous occasion a board had been placed
before a group of buildings, and a few days later she had received a laconic notice that it had disappeared, without any
reason for its loss being given.

In fact, our sign-boards certainly—and perhaps ourselves—
did not seem very welcome to the grey-haired, but young-
looking, lean and keen educator who received us. He was certainly all courtesy to us while all rudeness about the boards:
so perhaps he distinguished between the two.

He took Mrs. Michaelis aside and informed her—I gathered
afterwards—that the children's houses were not cages in a zoo
to be labelled with the names of the donors. The children

objected to them very strongly. Even if they didn't do so, such announcements could only harm them morally by pointing them out as objects of charity.

Perhaps I should not interpret here this conversation which was not meant for my ears. But it was so symptomatic of something about Israel, that it seems important to record it.

It all seemed a tremendous fuss about something rather unimportant. The harassed organizers of charity, after all, sometimes have to make concessions to the desires of donors to have the record of their gifts laid up on earth, in default of their having confidence that they will be duly noted in heaven. If early Renaissance painters, with their vivid Italian temperaments, could manage to include the portraits of donors in the corner of some tryptichs denoting the ranks of angels in heaven, I should have thought that an Israeli child could have put up with having his dormitory or schoolroom neatly labelled with the name and address of some fellow-Jews in Cincinnati or Connecticut, who had made it possible for him to sleep or work there.

However, such conflicts between Israeli and American Jews are a matter of almost everyday occurrence, and I kept on running into embarrassing examples of them. A few days later, a wealthy American visitor mentioned the following complaint to me. He had been going on a conducted tour of citreous and olive groves, when he happened to notice that some olives which were ripe had not been gathered. Wishing, perhaps, to show an intelligent interest, he asked the guide: "Why haven't those olives been picked?" The guide explained that there was a shortage of labour in this area. "But surely," said the American, "in a country as poor as this and with so many immigrants coming in, you could have arranged for someone to pick those olives?" The guide stopped the car, and said: "You can get out and pick them yourself, if you like." This, of course, is a single example but it points to the same attitude as I had noticed at Negbah.

Such absurd scenes, which crop up all the time, are the results of a complex relationship between the Israelis and the American Jews. The Israeli Jews, almost inevitably, believe that all Jews should return to the National Home. Not to do so, and not to realize that the Jew in the Diaspora is a stranger in a strange land, incurring if not to-day then certainly to-morrow, the loathing and active persecution of the foreigners by whom he is surrounded, is not only to ignore the teachings of the Bible and of Zionism, but to be the self-deceived victim of a glittering illusion. The Jews who to-day prosper in America are dwellers in a Babylon which is certain sooner or later to turn against them. Therefore, although one may be grateful for the gifts they send to Israel, it is impossible not to realize that these are only the means of buying off their consciousness of what is the real truth of the situation: that they should simply return, with all their belongings, to the Promised Land.

The newly erected children's buildings in Negbah were among the very best I saw anywhere in Israel. They were planned around a large square which at the present moment was of mud being planted with the shoots of trees and laid with pipes by children armed with spades and watering cans. In a few years this would be a beautiful parkland, sheltering clean white buildings of an architecture simple but exemplary, and exceptionally well-designed for Israel. At the lower end of this large square a pavilion-like building, under construction, was to be the school dining room.

"Is this all being built by members of the Kibbutz?" I asked—a little tactlessly.

"Of course," the lithe, grey-haired educator replied.

I noticed that he answered every question I put to him either with "of course," or "of course not."

In the case of the question I had just put, his terseness was understandable. I should have realized that the employing of hired labour from outside, is as much against the principles of the Kibbutzim, as is breaking the Sabbath to the Orthodox religious. Moreover, at present it is a highly delicate question; because the government, worried by the refusal of the new Eastern immigrants to go on to the land, have been trying to persuade the Kibbutzim to hire their labour. In some cases, the Kibbutzim have done so.

The educator took me into the children's class room—airy and light with windows on two sides. There were excellent biological, botanical and geographical charts on the walls and shelves along the sides of the room, with, on them, glass tanks and jars containing living and dead specimens.

The children, the teacher told me—with a touch of defiance, for Youth Aliyah dogma, I thought—worked six hours a day at their classes, two hours in the fields. (Youth Aliyah practice is four hours of each.) The Youth Aliyah Children and those from the Kibbutz went together to school up here. The Kibbutz children became so attached to their school life that after a time many of them did not take the trouble to walk down the hill to see their parents at the Kibbutz more often than once in a fortnight, he added, with a touch of pride.

He explained to me that the system of teaching was to make the children study by topics. For instance, if they were being taught about frogs, they would learn about the pond and the whole environment in which the frogs lived. Subjects were not divided up but grouped around particular objects of study.

Another feature of the system is to keep the children—as it were, at all costs—together in groups. The group arrive together, work together, live together; and the aim is that after their schooling is finished they should stay together. The intelligent are not promoted, the stupid (unless they are mentally defective candidates for the special homes) are not left behind. The group remains a solid, unbreakable unit. In this way they are trained to think and feel as members of the limited kind of community which is the Kibbutz. No marks are given ("of course not"), there are no examinations ("of course not"), and everything is done to prevent each child from putting himself

H

or any of the others into separate mental categories.

After I had been round the school, we walked down the hill
—with the great smooth view of the plain in front and over-
looked by the police fortress behind—to the Kibbutz, where
we sat in the beautiful clean dining room—with the sense of a
kitchen full of excellent utensils beyond—and ate oranges
while, full of curiosity, I questioned this intelligent and self-
assured educator about the Kibbutz life.

The members of the Kibbutz lead a life which is, as far as
possible, completely communal. It is the co-operative communism of the members of a small community who are agreed
as to aims and who watch one another perpetually, reasonably
and humanly, with a sense of what can be expected from and
what is required by, each one.

The only money that each member has is I£10 allowance
of pocket money for the week or ten days' holiday in a year
when he is away from the Kibbutz. A further small allowance
is made for the expenses of each child on holiday.

Everything you reasonably want is given to you when you
ask for it, and if the Kibbutz funds can provide it. You are a
chain smoker? Well, if cigarettes are necessary to you and the
community is in a position to provide them, you may be allowed
up to fifty a day.

Most members are given working clothes and recreation
clothes. "But as an educator who has to change often from
outdoor to indoor clothes, I am allowed some extra pairs of
trousers."

Each married couple has a room provided for them in a
semi-detached house consisting of only two rooms together
with simple but adequate furniture. No children are permitted to live in these houses. They have children's quarters
of their own, with communal nurseries and dormitories. They
do, however, visit their parents at the end of the day's work,
between five, when the parents get home from the fields, and
seven, when the children go to bed.

We went to visit the children in their clean white playroom, with little drawings pinned neatly in a line on one of the walls, and little toys scattered about. Some children were playing in an exemplary way (the younger ones who had gone to bed, were all beautifully tucked in and asleep). All the children looked clean, well and contented. The educator threw a cushion at one, and tugged at another. I noticed that they seemed less intimidated by him than I was.

As we went away, Mrs. Michaelis smiled and said: "Well, I must say I can't get my little David to go to sleep as soon as he's put to bed." My thoughts were running on the same lines.

I asked the educator: "Do you mean to say that the babies are taken away from their mothers and put into the communal quarters the moment they're born ?"

"Of course."

"Does any adult sleep in the children's dormitory at night to supervise them?"

"Of course not."

"But what happens during the night if a child is frightened or unwell?"

"It is the task of one girl to be up all night and supervise the dormitories."

"Are the children ever alone, in the evenings for example?"

"Of course not."

"How are their evenings organized?"

"Properly, of course. To-night, for instance, there will be chess. To-morrow, discussion. The next night there will be some kind of show. And so on."

He revealed that of all the adults in the community, about a third are, in one capacity or another, engaged in looking after the children. As far as I remember, this meant that two hundred were occupied in this way.

"Our trouble is that unless we get more members of the community, we won't have enough adults to work in the fields.

Unfortunately though, very few people apply to join. The new immigrants prefer to go the towns."

I asked him whether there were any artists in the community.

"Of course. There is a painter."

"When is he allowed to paint?" "For one day a week. The rest of the time, he works in the fields, like everyone else."

He took us to his charming, light, clean room with furniture provided by the Kibbutz, and books, because he was a teacher, and a few very small reproductions of paintings on the walls.

In the privacy of his room, I asked him what he thought about the arrest of Mr. Oren, the Mapam Party member, who, having been sent to attend an economic conference at Prague, as Mapam's special gesture of friendship to the East, was promptly arrested there. "What do I think about it?" he asked. "I don't give the matter a thought." "Why not?" Mrs. Michaelis asked. "We know nothing about it at present," he replied. "But no doubt Mr. Oren will return in a month's time, and then he will explain everything to us." "Do you really expect him to return?" I asked, surprised. "Of course. What do you imagine?" he asked, with a faintly superior smile. "Do you think he's been killed? Do you think they've hidden him away somewhere? There is nothing sinister about his arrest. There has doubtless been some mistake, and as soon as it is cleared up, he will return."

It is now several months since I wrote down this conversation, and—needless to say—Mr. Oren has not returned. Letters from the Israeli government asking Prague for some explanation of his arrest, are now no longer answered. I need hardly wonder what the educator at Nebgah is thinking, since it is more than likely that Mr. Oren's prolonged absence will in itself seem suspect and will have accustomed him to the idea of his guilt on some unspecified charge which, in its turn, will be explained in due course.

We left his room and he took me to see the clinic of the

Kibbutz, which was beautiful in every way, with a perfectly clean surgery, equipped with instruments and drugs, and a comfortable waiting room for patients. After seeing this I could say with conviction: "You really have something to be very proud of."

Negbah gave me a great deal to think about.

There is no doubt that it is a superb achievement. On the ruins of a place completely destroyed in the fighting, the members of this community have built a model settlement. It is a triumph of industry, good organization and ideals.

There is much to be said both for and against the Kibbutz policy of segregating the children. In part, at least, this arises out of necessity, though it is pushed to a point beyond what is merely necessary. The parents cannot attend to the children during the day, but, with a different system, they could of course sleep at home. It can be said, though, that they are better looked after in the Children's Quarters than they would be at home. Besides this, there is the greater architectural simplicity of planning the Kibbutz with general quarters for the children and quarters for adults which are never for more than two people.

An argument often heard in the Kibbutzim—which has enough truth in it to make most parents living in town pause in their criticism—is that the Kibbutz parents really devote their two hours each day to their children in a whole-hearted way. It is also pointed out that in families whose members are always all thrown together, parents and children often spend so much time avoiding one another that they certainly cannot be said to be really together for as much as two hours each day.

The best reply to the Kibbutz system (in its extreme form, as practised at Negbah) comes from other Kibbutzim where to-day plans are being made to arrange for the children to sleep in their parents' quarters; or from other settlements which try to work out a way of life which will solve some of the problems ignored by most Kibbutzim. Lionel Feitelberg, in a

pamphlet describing an experiment in communal living at
*Moledeth Bnei Brith, writes:

> "In the Kibbutz . . . the relations between the children and
> the parents are purely of a social and sentimental character—
> the child lives his routine life with all its duties and pleasures,
> apart from his parents; and as they, too, are only part of the
> larger organization which the child sees around him, he cannot
> really feel that he shares any real part of their real life either.
> The family meets in its leisure hours, and the relationship between
> the various members is one of love and pleasure, without any of
> the troubles that the full twenty-four-hour-day cycle inevitably
> brings in private life, and without any of the personal responsi-
> bility which families in individual life come to feel for the sur-
> vival of the family. In the Moshav, on the other hand, the child
> from his earliest years, is a responsible member of the family."

That the children have too much a recreation-time relationship with their parents in the Kibbutz, and do not realize
sufficiently the routine of their lives, seems a just criticism,
which also applies (though differently) to English upper class
families where the children are sent away to boarding school
at the age of seven or eight. This criticism is not really met by
the favourite Kibbutz argument that the parents and children
are devoted to one another during these two hours.

Dr. Dux, when I raised Mrs. Y——'s criticisms about the
thumb-sucking children of the Kibbutzim, had said: "The
children don't only suck their thumbs. They also bed-wet.
One can't, alas, say that there are fewer insecure children in
the Kibbutzim than in the towns."

"The other day," he said, "I saw a child in one of these
play-rooms with his thumb in his mouth and, with a very
disturbed manner, I asked: 'Where are your parents?'

"He said: 'My father is a truck-driver. My mother has gone
to the town to teach in a seminar. I am nearly always alone
except when I am at school.'

"Things like this often happen in the Kibbutzim. School is

---

*Moledeth Bnei Brith, by Lionel Feitelberg, Palestine Pioneer Library, No.16

over by four in the afternoon. The children are then supposed
to go and visit their parents. But often the child goes and finds
no parents, or only one, and then he asks where is the other.

"Remember too that often the child comes home at exactly
the same time as the parents, and then he realizes that no one
is at home most of the day. Or sometimes the parents have
only just returned home, and they are tired. But the children
want to play.

"However, all cases aren't like this. In the majority of cases
even when the situation is as I describe it, the children are
well."

> I met a little seven years child,
>   His thumb was in his mouth:
> "Why are you thus disturbed," I asked
>   "My pretty little youth?"

> "My father is a truck driver,
>   My mother at the seminar.
> So oft when I come home from school,
>   My parents are afar.

> "Or when I meet them at our door
>   They're tired after their heavy day.
> In the two hours when I'm at home,
>   They are too tired to play."

An Israeli Wordsworth, writing his Lyrical Ballads would
have to devise a moral for this problem. Perhaps his best line
of defence of the Kibbutz would be that the children belong to
a family whose parents are the whole community. For the
members of the Kibbutz are often as much bound to the community as most husbands and wives in marriage. The children,
in their relationship to this communal parentage have more
pressure brought on them not to go away from the home of the
Group, than is brought on the children of the outside world
not to leave their parents.

For me, the most disturbing thing about Negbah was that
it combined achievements which I could only admire with

theoretical attitudes with which I could not agree, especially when these touched on the political structure of the outside world.

Is it possible that these people, living within the margins of their limited excellence, make the mistake of judging the world by the standards of their Kibbutz? Communism works excellently when everyone knows and trusts everyone else, though even here it leads to the breaking-up of the group if there is serious disagreement on some principle. But it becomes an entirely different thing when the committees which direct it are dogmatists laying down rules of thinking, taskmasters demanding work to achieve the ends of the states, and dealers-out of material goods according to a rule based not on knowledge of each separate individual, but on what are supposed to be average needs of abstract, average people.

The educator to whom I spoke, evidently expected the Communist leaders in Prague to know all about Mr. Oren, as though he were a member of their own Kibbutz, who might for a few days be the victim of a misunderstanding, but who could also be certain that this would be cleared up before long.

Yet the over-confident application of the standards of the Kibbutz to politics has struck back at the Kibbutzim themselves by causing such bitter disagreement between members who cannot tolerate one another's views, that many settlements have broken into seceding groups.

CHAPTER IX

MODERN TOWN AND OLD VILLAGE

T EL-AVIV is an entirely modern town, built on the hopeless looking sand dunes. It lies like a great half of a cartwheel, or like a spider-web, with radiating and criss-cross roads, upon the shore of white sand against the blue canvas of the sea. The sea-front is a wide, straight, long boulevard with houses which look like the backs of buildings facing the sea, the road across a wide esplanade. This shabby pierless Brighton reaches south to Jaffa, and the north is divided from the sea by a wedge of ramshackle wooden tenements right on the beach.

It is a town of abortive sky-scrapers perched on hidden stilts, with piles sunk into the sand under the dunes.

Most of the buildings are as much exiles from the Germany of the Weimar Republic as some of the inhabitants. "Here," they seem to say, "by the blue sea, we have planted the ideas of Gropius and Mendelssohn, in a perfect desert of empty whiteness. Here, if anywhere, the soulless, heartless modern architecture, without decorations, without body and without bones, ought to be able to prove that beauty can be completely abstract to a sun that stares on it without comment and without interruption."

Like all modern architecture, this has the quality of egg shells. As long as the egg shells look perfectly white they are strongholds of pure form, reflecting only light. But let one bird dropping fall on them, one bit of down from a real chicken cling to their surface, one crack appear, one wash of dirty water cover them, and their cold virginity violated for ever,

115

they look depraved as prostitutes. And that is what Tel-Aviv looks like: a town of buildings which are architectural whores. But that is the fault of the architecture only. The town itself has the respectability of the rest of Israel. It is untainted by pleasure—or almost so.

Hidden away at the back of the town, five blocks from the sea, is the Rothschild Boulevard, a soughing memory of the part of the Kurfürstendamm which almost adjoins the Gedaechtniskirche.

With a double-row of trees stretching down the centre of it, and a park-like carpet in the middle of that—and traffic going in opposite directions on either side—at night the Rothschild Boulevard, with windows opening on to scented boughs, and square box-like roofs against the stars, does seem to whisper of Central Europe—Vienna even. Leaves stretch their fingers like gloved hands of slender women against a diamonded sky. Voices murmur from the interiors of rooms as from carved violins. But during the day, the Rothschild Boulevard looks shabby and uninteresting, lost under the too-large sky.

All the same, Tel-Aviv does have something. It has magnificent situation, like a stage facing the sea, which seems made for a great city. At a first glance Tel-Aviv may look like the most monumental record of all the errors of modern architecture. At a second glance, the visitor feels merely that he has arrived too soon. It is a scene partly not ready, partly needing reconstruction, botched with mistakes which can, though, be deleted. The streets are broad and well planned and most of the houses have the merit of looking easy to pull down.

At sunset, the sea front faces a view of the sun at the exact centre of a horizon framed between trees, a sun standing upon the charcoaled line of the horizon, above which the sky is all fire, and below which the sea is polished metal.

In April at midnight, standing upon a roof in the centre of the city you can smell the inundating scent of orange trees, borne upon the breezes blowing out to sea.

Twenty years ago, Tel-Aviv scarcely existed, and twenty years hence, it will doubtless be an immense city. Its air of having a future is one of the things that add faith to Israel, and that is doubtless why many people who must be aware of its ugliness find it the most encouraging of all the towns in which to live. It goes its own gregarious perverse way, growing up where no one ever expected there to be a city, accumulating more and more crowds who simply want to be there, people who build and somehow prosper. That is how many cities came into being, which have borne countries upon their unreasoning shoulders. It is still the centre of unplanned vitality in planned Israel. Ideal villages in which immigrants are beneficially placed empty overnight, and their inhabitants lose themselves among the populace of Tel-Aviv.

To-day Tel-Aviv is filled with a population more and more Oriental in appearance. The crowds on the sea shore look decidedly like those of a Levantine town. At moments the sea front seems to connect with the great boulevard of Bombay.

The branch of Hadassah in Tel-Aviv, under the auspices of Mrs. Davidowitz, wife of the translator of Shakespeare into Hebrew, arranged for me to go to Ben Shemen, one of the oldest settlements to which children have been brought. It is made famous above all by the presence of Dr. Siegfried Lehmann who brought with him a group of children into this part of the country, surrounded by Arab villages, as early as 1927.

Ben Shemen is a charming, tree-shadowed place, which has spread outwards around an old farm house. Its buildings, considerably shattered by the war, are of a more leisurely style of frame architecture than those of the newer villages.

The farmer, owner of the farm and now aged 90, is still there among his hens and cows, called "grandpa" by the children who have grown up around him. The main part of the village is grouped around four or five quadrangles with gardens in them. It has the greatest variety of trees I saw even in Israel, the most frequent being cedars and palm trees.

I was taken to see Dr. Lehmann who very kindly invited me to stay at his house. This wooden-frame little building, behind a fence over which the leaves of banana trees spread like fans, and with a flat roof-garden from which there is a wonderful view of the surrounding plains, is like a fairy-tale home for two of the best-loved persons in Israel, Siegfried Lehmann and his doctor wife.

Downstairs, Dr. Lehmann has a study and a dining room, pleasantly opening into one another. His study was almost completely book-lined except where there were frames of beautiful reproductions of Florentine paintings. The dining room was panelled with a light-coloured wood. His surroundings were those of a man of learning and a lover of beauty.

He sat in an armchair. He looked far from well and got up painfully to greet me. Then he returned to his chair, drawing a rug over his knees. He had the expression of one who does work which requires close-looking: a village shoe-mender, a scholar of Chinese, or a worker in precious stones.

His conversation was somehow so characteristic of himself— with many parentheses—which contributed to his main subject, of which he never lost sight, despite his often disjointed sentences, that I have attempted to reproduce his manner of talking, hoping that it will convey some impression of the charm of the man himself.

He talked about his own life, because I put questions which asked him to do so. He told me that he began by being the director of a settlement for Jewish children in the working class quarters of Berlin. Then he went to Lithuania, where he became adviser in child welfare.

In 1927 he brought to Israel one hundred children from Kaunas Children's Home and here he began to build the Children's Village.

The children took part in the building of their own houses.

"My idea was that we should have difficult children and then put them into a stream of activity and let them be carried by it.

"Not that the children from Lithuania were difficult . . ." he corrected himself with characteristic scrupulousness. "From the land we took difficult. . . . You see our idea was that if the children were active then they would be carried along by their activity. . . ."

He stopped and looked with a gleaming glance and a smile— in the manner with which I quickly grew familiar, not distracting me, but strangely deepening his effect, and said: " I remember an example—a boy of twelve who was taken up by the police. Let's see, that must have been in 1934. A terrible background. The father had married twice, and the stepmother hadn't allowed the boy home at night. The boy slept on the steps outside his home. This boy was specially difficult. A cruel case. Then he'd also had an illness on his scalp during the war, and they'd given him too strong a dose of the X-ray which was used, and he'd lost all his hair. It weighed terribly on the boy that he'd had this illness. He learned nothing, stuck to no work, and, worst of all, he was a bed-wetter. We thought we'd give him a chance. If we brought him here, the influence of this country might make him a different boy. He came, and he had—that was interesting—two assets. He could draw and he was musical. We taught him to play the violin, and drawing. When he was satisfied with himself—that is perhaps worth mentioning—psychologically interesting—when he was satisfied with himself, he didn't bed-wet. When he was unhappy, he did. . . .

"Think . . . It wasn't as though he was alone in one room at home. How dreadful for such a boy, with three companions in a room. But we were already on the way. Naturally, he stole— stole badly—but *es ging*—it went.

"I remember—how it all comes back to me !—there was a festival, the *purim*. That was quite a shocking scene. In that evening the boy had a wonderful dress. . . . He used to dress like that wonderfully once a year. . . . And—*merkwürdig*—he has put on a wig. He was dressed as a page. This was the one night in the year when he was a beautiful boy. . . . Oh, we had a prince among us.

"Then a misfortune occurred. . . . The other children improvised poems. It was gay at midnight, the boy was sixteen. Each of the children made up verses about some other child. It was all good-humoured, really perfectly good-humoured. One boy—no, not at all out of bad will, but just for fun—made a verse about this boy, and in the verse there was a reference to his bed-wetting.

"The boy went back to his room." Dr. Lehmann threw up his hands, and smiled almost. "All we hoped we'd attained was lost. He didn't want to stay with us any longer. We helped get him a place as apprentice to a carpenter. Interesting, his last conversation with me. In this last conversation. . . ."

At this point the telephone rang. With difficulty he got up and crossed the room to answer it. Then he came back and continued the sentence exactly where he'd left off.

". . . he said: 'I will come back to Ben Shemen when I can really play.' (On Friday evening we always have concerts.) 'They will all be sitting in the twilight with the candles burning on the tables, and then suddenly the bed-pisser' (I remember he used that coarse phrase) 'will come in and will take up his violin. And then all the children will know what he was really like'."

"And did he come back and play the violin as he said?" I interrupted, wanting the story to end this way.

Dr. Lehmann shook his head, and smiled his bright, sharp, scrutinizing smile.

"Well, soon after he left us, he also left the carpenter to whom we had apprenticed him. Never had a job for longer than six months. At nineteen he had sunk terribly. He frequented brothels. Was utterly impoverished. Completely fallen.

"Then the change came in this boy at twenty or twenty-one

years. Perhaps that was a little due to us—we tried to give him a vocation in which his artistic sense was bound up with a handicraft. Well, to-day, he's a man with a family and children. From the boy, a man. And then a specialist in the theatre. Theatrical design. Drawing helped him in the theatre. And, of course, no one round him knowing anything about his past. Not one thing.

"This wasn't the only case we'd believed to be quite hopeless. His father syphilitic. What we learned was to be patient. There are quite a lot of these cases which the teacher thinks are hopeless. The lesson for the teacher is that the pupil's hopelessness is not his excuse for giving up. The boy's artistic gift was what really saved him. . . .

"Yes, yes, one calls other cases now to mind.

"A girl whom no amount of affection could help. Went to Cairo. Never came back. This Cairo girl was from here, she was an Israeli, not from Kaunas. I want to make it clear to you that sometimes we've succeeded, sometimes not.

"When I try to draw conclusions about our whole experience, I think that sometimes we——. I tell you, I don't want to be too explicit. But I think that with a good many of the children we've——. But certainly also. And there again. I'd like to.

"See, at fourteen, a boy is a bud coming out. The hereditary father only breaks through at seventeen—for good or for bad. To make a prognosis, we should take into account the two ages, fourteen and then also seventeen. One can make bad mistakes at fourteen. Children at that age are often geniuses. It is the genius of puberty—with a charm—with such potentialities it deceives. Then suddenly—after puberty—he becomes a bourgeois. The problem is all contained in these intervening years between fourteen and seventeen.

"The cases I've mentioned are, though, exceptional. There remain the thousands of cases of those who simply go on the stream which takes them into the Kibbutzim or the town. The examples I gave you are extremes."

I asked him on what principle they decided whether students should enter the Kibbutzim or go to the towns. He explained that they had a vocational training centre at Kfar Vitkin, known as the "new Ben Shemen," some miles away, on the coast. There the children learned mechanical agriculture—use of tractors—carpentry, electricity, and tailoring.

He showed me with pride some of the things in his room: the Moroccan carpets, the covers on the furniture, and some of the furniture itself, and said that all these were from the school workshop, made by the children, and presented to him at various times.

"We want to give everyone the chance to be a *Landarbeiter* (agriculturist). But if he's not suited to this, then we mustn't make a mistake. We must give him the chance to be a *Handwerker* (artisan)."

I asked him whether they encouraged the teaching of art. He said that they had a considerable collection of children's drawings which had been used in psychical therapy. But all the archives had been destroyed during the fighting.

"Let's admit," he said, "that we haven't gone in so much for sport here. The children do it, but other places do more and are better at it. However, we have achieved a lot in music. Why, we have had here a wonderful musician, Chanan Eisenstadt, a man to whom the children really respond. He is a one-armed pianist—a villager and a great artist. Because the children love him so immensely, we've been able to have a children's orchestra. Our favourite composer here is Handel. . . . But Gluck also . . .

"On every Friday evening for 33 years, we've had music done by teachers and children with different instruments.

"Yes, Handel is our . . ." Now I find his German gaining on me so that I noted what he was saying in the German. *"Ich glaube, das Musik überhaupt das Mittel zur Ehrfurcht ist.* I think music the means above all of attaining—" But how exactly can *Ehrfurcht* be translated? We discussed this a while. In German,

perhaps *the sacred*. "Or, better still, the sense of that which is
quite other than we are. *Musik ist vielleicht das Einzige heute.*
To-day music is perhaps the only means of attaining this.

"There are moments when nothing is sacred to children.
Other moments when all is sacred.

"So we had music on Friday evenings, then a reading from
the Bible. First it was very difficult to keep them waiting for
their food. Imagine. After the day's work the children go into
the dining room and see the tables laid, with bread placed on
them—and then they have to wait. Soon they learned to be
silent. With silence everything can begin.

"Yes, religion. At the Sabbath Feast the same boys—
geschworene Feinde, determined enemies of religion—take
part and sing with—if I can make it clear why—and sing also
the religious songs.

"Certain preliminaries necessary. Twilight. Many candles on
the tables. Singing songs with *Ehrfurcht*. Singing together. A
teacher says something. Then we sing together till the darkness
falls. Sing into the darkness. Then the lighting of the candles.

"If I ask myself—why do the children join in together?
Because there's a need—a need for something quite different.
Something which is not daily life.

"In the beginning, of course, there was a great deal of protest.
The irreligious ones, who were the majority, had a committee
to establish a programme for Friday evenings with songs and
stories. For a month or so we had socialist songs, or nature
songs. After a month, the children saw that we could do that
also on Wednesdays or Thursdays.

"You know about the agnostic Marxist movement here?
And you know about Mapai and Mapam? The development of
the settlement in a way so as to make it possible for the two to
live together in the one place, has not been easy for the two
parties. But we have both tendencies here. We saw much value
in this decision to stay together.

"My chief aim now . . . don't you think that the Word in

education . . . through too much diffusion of radio and news-papers . . . has lost worth? Then my aim is—instead of words—to put symbols. Lighted candles—silence before music—sunset—at the hour of the Sabbath Feast's beginning—that the silence and the twilight fall at the same moment upon the senses of the waiting children.

"My other aim is what it has always been—to combat chauvinism and to try to create understanding of the Arabs within our educational system. Before the war, Ben Shemen was surrounded with Arab villages. I deliberately chose the situation for that reason."

Dr. Lehmann said that the attitude of the English authorities unfortunately had not helped him in his attempts to work for Arab-Jewish understanding. He gave it as an example of the attitude of the British authorities that in 1935, when he had managed to get both Arab and Jewish teachers to agree to attend a meeting in order to discuss their common problems in teaching, the British forbade this meeting.

"In 1941, we arranged to devote a week here to Arab culture. We had an exhibition of Arab clothes and art, and Arab children came from the surrounding country and performed their dances. When the Education Director of the Mandatory Government heard that the Arab teachers were taking part in this, he was very uneasy. Perhaps the Government thought that meetings between Arab and Jewish teachers must imply some sort of Communist intrigue.

"After this, though, we arranged classes here for Arab child-ren, in carpentry. Once we had a meeting of two classes. The children of thirteen from an Arab class, and our class. The children sat in their class-room together. A thirteen-year-old fellaheen next to one of our thirteen-year-old girls. Our children danced their dances, and they danced ours."

In nothing that Dr. Lehmann said was there the slightest trace of bitterness: which there well might have been, as one of the actions of the Mandatory Government had been to imprison him for some weeks. The circumstances in which this occurred are reported in Arthur Koestler's *Promise and Fulfilment* :

"During the autumn of 1939 and the spring of 1940, British Police and Army swooped down on Jewish settlements and Haganah training camps, confiscated their arms and arrested the leaders. The most notable of these actions was directed against the Judaean settlement of Ben Shemen, which served as an agricultural boarding-school for 450 refugee children from 6 to 17 years of age. It had repeatedly been attacked by Arab gangs. In January 1940 a Police search unearthed 27 rifles, 5 submachine-guns with ammunition and 23 grenades concealed under a tiled floor. On April 22 a British military court sentenced eight members of the staff to prison terms ranging from three to seven years. There was no suggestion even on the part of the prosecution that the arms were intended for any purpose other than for defending the school against recurrent Arab attacks. The prosecution was in fact careful to point out that no aggressive intentions were imputed to the staff, but that the letter of the law had to be respected."

In 1947, there was a second disaster, when on December 15th a supply convoy proceeding to Ben Shemen was ambushed, and fourteen Jews were killed. After this the children had to be evacuated. Dr. Lehmann gave me the impression of never having quite reconciled himself to this. He spoke of the ambush as though it were a misunderstanding, or at any rate, an occurrence which he thought would not have happened again.

Ben Shemen was one of the most moving places I visited in Israel. That evening I met some of Dr. Lehmann's staff, and talked with them. Wonderful as the work still being done there is, it gave me an impression of sadness. Dr. Lehmann himself was ill, too much had been destroyed in the war, and now it was involved in the financial crisis of the whole of Israel, just at a time when even in more prosperous circumstances it would have needed aid to achieve recovery. Nothing struck me as sadder than that so much of Dr. Lehmann's work should have fallen into decay around him.

Promise and Fulfilment, by Arthur Koestler, Macmillan, 1949.

CHAPTER X

THE ITALIAN VILLAGE

Aꜰᴛᴇʀ this I went northwards by slow stages as far as the northernmost point of the Jordan—a place of waters surrounded by tremendous trees—near Dan. The source of the river, a few hundred yards still further north, is in Arab territory.

The northern country, dominated by Mount Hermon, and sloping through many foothills down to the Sea of Tiberias, is the most beautiful part of this beautiful country. The hills are smoother, greener, more polished than the stony hills around Jerusalem. There are many high plateaux above the wide, luxuriant, dark-soiled Jordan valley, high above which you see forever Hermon, snow-capped and held in the sky above Israel—a moon-gleaming beacon above the dim dark sleeve of its high slopes.

The Sea of Tiberias is approached from Safed, to the north of the lake, by a road which skirts hilly meadows on the slope traditionally supposed to be the place of the Sermon on the Mount.

The ochre, blue and green colours of this part of the country, with its wide views under a great sky, are like glass in which colour reflects colour under the bright sunlight. The lake itself, seen from a distance, absorbs so much of the colours of the hills, that its own blueness often seems cancelled: part of the lake seems swept through by the golden yellow of rocks, another part by the green of fields, while the rest is pure black and white.

Across the Jordan are the glowing hills of Arab territory,

126

glimmering like shot silk, with lines of fields and rocks faint yet perfect through the atmosphere, diamonded with the colours of harlequin. It is a land which stretches across mountains and deserts into the depths of Asia.

West of the Sea of Tiberias is Nazareth, spread out over the hills. Its stone, square-built houses which seem like a terracing of the hills with rock, are Arab in character, hardly influenced by the rash of monasteries, churches and monuments which has grown around the Holy Places. The town is part Christian, part Arab, part Jewish.

For some reason the guides who show you round the Holy Places are Arab, though this does not seem to affect their credulity about Christian wonders. In the crypt of the Church of the Annunciation, built over an old basilica, supposedly erected by St. Helena and Constantine in the Fourth Century, we were shown the cave-dwelling supposedly the house of the Virgin Mary, and in other places other things equally famous. The Holy Places are the *reductio ad absurdum* of tourism. It is as though people should travel hundreds of miles to see galleries consisting of pictures not only uninteresting in themselves, but known to be fakes, or to be shown a damp patch on the wall which someone totally untrustworthy had once claimed to be a Leonardo, or a piece of shapeless stone thought to have been left about by Michelangelo.

Perhaps though people really go to Nazareth because the name itself is sanctified, because the town is beautiful, and because it has an Arab life, with a market, narrow streets, and people in Arab dress. Certainly what is left of Arab life to-day in Israel comes on the senses with an extraordinary feeling of relaxation, grace and refreshment. It is nice to see architecture which seems to grow out of the landscape, houses as much a part of nature as the stones around Jerusalem, and people dressed—and not just undressed—to suit the climate.

One of the most curious places in Israel is the beautiful remains of a Synagogue on the Northern shore of the Sea of

Tiberias, at *Tel Ham*, the New Testament Capernaum. This synagogue was built by a Roman centurion friendly to the Jews, and it is supposedly the one in which Jesus often preached. It is a combination of the Greek, the Roman and the Jewish which makes one realize how different civilizations drew together at times in the disinterested minds of Roman governors. With its ornamentation in which the acanthus leaf of the Corinthian column is set beside the star of David and different symbolic fruits, it is like an architectural statement of Pilate's question: "What is truth?" A screen of beautiful trees, hiding and revealing the flashing waters, divides the Synagogue from the lake.

Safed, in the mountains of the Upper Galilee, is beloved by the Israelis as the most beautiful resort in Israel. Many artists live there (not a very good omen for Israeli art, as it is usually a mistake for artists to live in very beautiful places). This city with its white houses crowds on the summit of a hill 3,000 feet high, with wonderful views on every side has many narrow lanes running down the hillside between houses which are famous for their exquisite courtyards.

Safed is admired for the blue light which reflects from the cloudless skies on to its white walls. It is also a place revered in the hearts of Jews because Jewish scholars and mystics of the Kabbala have worked here uninterruptedly for many centuries.

It has added to its glory in recent years by what is called the "miracle of Safed" when, during the war the Jews, who were less than a quarter of the whole population of about 14,000 held out for weeks against the Arabs and finally won, partly, it is said by spreading a rumour that Haganah were masters of a secret atom bomb. There is a full and interesting account of this fighting in Koestler's *Promise and Fulfilment*.

Safed is now emptied of its Arabs, but I went to one predominantly Arab place, the lovely village of Peki'in. The members of this village are mostly Druses, Moslems and

Christians, and there is only one Jewish family. It is situated in Western Galilee just beyond a point in the road running over a mountain pass, where there is an immense view stretching on the one side as far as the Mediterranean, on the other to the Sea of Tiberias.

At the outskirts of the village we were greeted noisily by crowds of excited Arab children, who were occupied in making basket-work which they tried to sell us. But despite the noise, and the fact that Jews are regarded as foreigners in this place, there is a certain tranquillity about its inhabitants who are perhaps influenced by the beautiful square with the fountain under the branches of a great tree, the steep views seen all round at the top of steps leading to low-roofed houses, and at the sharp turnings at the end of streets.

The Arabs may be very backward, but in being so there are things which they have not lost. One of these is a style of architecture. They can build to-day an edifice exactly as they would have built it a thousand years ago, without its revealing that decadence of style or that vulgarity of pastiche which occurs when more "advanced" builders do the same thing. Or perhaps in the Tyrol, in Scandinavia, in Switzerland and—oddly, as it always strikes me—in America, Westerners can build wooden houses in a style not much altered through many hundreds of years. But we certainly can't be traditionally conventional on a great scale—as, say, with a cathedral: and our attempts to be traditional and yet modern seem doomed to failure. But, as I noticed at Acre—and had noticed previously in Cairo—here are a people who in the Eighteenth and Nineteenth Centuries (as perhaps also to-day) build mosques which—to put it in our terms—have the simplicity of Norman Cathedrals. Yet the modern mosques do not seem in the least anachronisms. The idea that a modern building must in some way express the changed attitude of civilization in recent years does not seem to have affected the consciousness of the Arabs.

After I had seen Acre, Safed and Peki'in it struck me how

little sense most Israelis seem to have of something lost in their country—the architectural tradition that existed there. Occasionally I heard someone express a nostalgia for the Arabs in the towns, with their headdresses, their camels and all their picturesque appurtenances. But I never heard anyone regret the Arab villages laid in ruins which one sees alongside every country road and of which there must be scores.

Perhaps though, the Jews have other losses to think about, I reflected when, on the way to Peki'in from Acre, I stopped to look at Lokhmey-ha-gettaoth, the Kibbutz "Fighters of the Ghetto." Here there is a museum of Concentration Camps, with frightful records of starvation, gas chambers, ovens, burial grounds, death trains, arrests, anti-Semitic proclamations, and all the horrible methods and propaganda of the anti-semitism which has wiped out six million Jews in the past twelve years. When you look at these records the whole modern world seems to disappear through doors of horror into meaninglessness. The children from the Kibbutz wandered indoors out of the sunlight into these dark rooms, without seeming aware of the albums on the table, the pictures on the walls.

In Jerusalem, someone mentioned to me that there was a village in the North where Italians had settled. He said that a Catholic peasant in a village near Foggia, after reading the Old Testament, had converted all the others to become Jews. At the time of their conversion, they had not realized that there were other Jews in the world. Later, they had got into touch with the Jewish community in Italy, had come to Israel, and were now regarded as among the most orthodox Jews in the country.

The story interested and amused me, so I decided to visit the converts. One reason for making the journey was my longing, whenever I have the opportunity, to see Italians and gain through them a little of the feeling of their country.

Alma—the village where the Italians had settled—lies at

the end of eight miles of execrable road in the Galilean hills, not far from Safed. Where the road to Alma branches off from the main road, we picked up an old man, in Druse dress, and with a white beard, and his grandson who accompanied him. They told us that there were only 12 Italian Jewish families in the village, the rest of whose members were Tunisians.

The first person we met when we came to the village was a small round-faced boy with blue eyes and fair hair, and a lively, amused expression. We told him we wanted to see "the Italians." He understood at once and said he would take us to his mother, who turned out to be the animator of the religious life of the group. The boy's name was David Bonfitto, and he was 10 or 12 years old.

We drove along what seemed a large common or pasture of grassland, until we came to the clean white new houses of Alma, at the edge of a plateau, beyond which was the wide gulf of the Jordan Valley. The brimming over snow-cap of Mount Hermon was elevated like the Host in the sky. It seemed only connected to the land by a slight darkening of the light like a faintly exposed part of a transparent negative.

The druse and his grandson got out, and David Bonfitto got into the back of the car, and answered our questions, telling us about the Italians and the Tunisians. We passed a donkey and Mr. Melitz, who accompanied me on this trip, asked: "Does the donkey talk Italian too?" "No," said David promptly, "only the Tripolitan dialect."

He took us to his mother's house, which had sky-blue walls inside and a living room opening into a slightly smaller bedroom. There were coloured prints, illustrating Jewish religious subjects on the walls.

Mr. Melitz looked at these, and murmured: "Images on the walls. That is not so orthodox."

In the further room, over the matrimonial double bed, there was a long large framed Hebrew inscription. David pointed to it proudly, and said: "I did that."

Signora Bonfitto was a middle-aged peasant woman, with rather square features and frizzy hair, and shining eyes like dark stones. She welcomed us and at once called in the other members of the family. She then gave orders to another woman —her sister, I think—and they prepared a dish of sweets with small portions of chocolate for us. We tried to refuse these morsels, but she had a kind of authority in offering them which compelled us to accept.

The sister, with her straight narrow features and long oval face, looked very much the spinster aunt. She wore a pendant round her neck: the Old Testament in enamel, opened at the Ten Commandments.

By now the room had filled up with about 10 people besides ourselves, among them two babies and two pretty young women, a middle-aged man wearing a beret, who had austere features and a frowning forehead; and a much younger man with toothbrush moustache and hair brushed back, who lolled easily on a chair, leaning its back against the wall, while he watched the proceedings with an air of detachment.

Signora Bonfitto sat in the midst of her little group with an air of waiting to say her piece. I asked her why she had come to Israel, and immediately she blazed forth into a prophetess. She clasped her hands together and shook them at the ceiling, raising her eyes. A torrent of Southern Italian dialect poured out of her, in which I could only recognize a few words, such as "the Holy Book," "Jerusalem" and "Prophet." She was like a medium in a trance.

I tried to stop her, without much effect. Then I turned to the others, explaining that I could not understand a word of what she was saying. This had its effect. Her family took my side in stopping her. Someone gave her a good shake, and she was quiet at once, merely looking round at us with distraught eyes, waiting to burst forth again. The rest of us consulted what to do about my inability to hear her. She waited, but with an air—as though to say we must decide, this had nothing

to do with her. We agreed that she should speak Italian, which
David would translate into Hebrew, which Mr. Melitz would
then translate in turn for me.

With this settled, I took up my note book. Seeing which,
David started off his functions by saying to Melitz: "Tell him
he'll never have enough paper to write down all she's going to
say." This was translated to me and also back to his mother in
Italian. She smiled and suddenly became quite human, cupping
David's face with her hand, and saying "*caro*," in the affection-
ate Italian way.

Then she settled back into her formidable pose—with her
grizzled disordered hair which framed her face, looking like
a wild halo—and started to tell her story. From time to time she
was interrupted by members of her family. They corrected her,
not very respectfully, I thought. After a few moments of
altercation, she would start up again. Occasionally her relatives
seemed to agree very profoundly with what she was saying,
and nodded their warm approval. It was obvious that they had
been summoned to her room because a recital to strangers of
her story was a kind of ritual for them. We were witnessing
the creation of a legend which was still in the formative stage
when relatives can chip in and correct the version coming hot
from the mouth of an evangelist.

In Garganico, the village near Foggia from which these
Italians came, there had lived a man called Donato Manduzzio.
Donato had a vision. In this vision he heard a voice. The voice
said: "Levi must light the lamp." Donato (in his dream) protested: "I haven't any matches." The voice replied : "It doesn't
matter. Your name is Levi, and you have to light the lamp."

After this dream, Donato obtained a copy of the Bible. And
he read it from cover to cover.

He saw that the first part of it—the Old Testament—con-
tained a message utterly different from the New Testament.
He said: "There are two religions, one Catholic and one
Protestant, both calling themselves Christian. Both are wrong.

The true religion is that contained in the Old Testament."

So he started trying to persuade the other members of his village to share his views. He told them they were idolators who worshipped the graven images of the Virgin, and of her Son.

Most of the Christians—Signora Bonfitto went on—said Donato was a fool. Donato said: "You rest on Sunday. But God said you should rest on Saturday: on the Sabbath, not on Sunday." And they all made jokes about him, and mocked.

She herself then read the Old and the New Testaments. "I decided that Donato was right," she said quietly: And she added, amidst a silence which was impressive: "So I broke the statues."

Everyone—even the young man with the tooth-brush moustache—was a little awed when she said this.

Signora Bonfitto interrupted her narrative now, to ask David to fetch something from the next room. He came back a moment later with a silken cloth, as large as a table cloth. He spread this out and showed it to us. Embroidered on it were the Ten Commandments. They were done in a pale grey silk as though with the purpose of making the lettering—which was very beautiful, resembling that on a Roman Triumphal Arch— almost invisible. The Commandments were in Italian and printed all in capitals.

When we had finished looking at the cloth, she continued her story.

All this while, she said, Donato and his followers were ignorant that there were other Jews than themselves in the world.

One day a pedlar came to the village. Donato told the pedlar of his ideas, and the pedlar said: "There are many people who think as you do. They are called Jews. And that is what you are —a Jew. If you like I will give you the address of another Jew. He lives in Naples."

So Donato—who now had adopted the name of Levi given to him in his dream—wrote to this address. And the Jew in

Naples wrote back sending the name and address of the Rabbi in Rome. But there was no answer to his letter. "The Rabbi thought we were joking—that it was all a practical joke that we were amusing ourselves with."

Here the young man with the toothbrush moustache, put his chair up straight, smiled at me and murmured, rather affectionately, and softly, as though to himself: " A practical joke!"

Signora Bonfitto continued: "We wrote again to Rome, and still got no answer.   Three times we had to write before we got a reply. Then, finally, the Rabbi wrote to Donato: 'I thought you were joking, but now I see you really want to become a Jew'."

After this, the Rabbi sent a representative to Garganico. This man, who came from Rome, didn't say a word. He came only to listen. He stayed a whole day with Levi, only listening. Then, when he was leaving he made one remark, which was: "You are more a Jew than all the other Jews." And he saw Signora Bonfitto's cloth with the Ten Commandments embroidered on it, and he said: " I see you are a Jewess also."

Books were despatched from Rome to the village. At this point in the narrative, David was sent out to the next room to fetch these also. They were simple books of instruction in the Jewish religion, written in Italian.

Now a whole succession of visitors started arriving from Rome. One of them was a Jewish historian who "came to see the great light which was shining in Garganico."

On another occasion, when a famous Hebrew scholar was taking his leave, the villagers said to him: "Won't you give us something to remember your visit by?"

He said: "You need no souvenir from me. You have a prophet, a Jewish prophet, amongst you."

Before his death, Levi knew already of the existence of the Jewish State, since it had been declared. He knew then that his body could not, but that his soul would, return to his homeland. On his deathbed he had a dream about a flock of sheep and a voice which said: "This flock is going back to its home and this flock is of the people of Israel."

After Donato died, Signora Bonfitto did not know what would be the future of the Jews at Garganico. But then she also started having dreams. In the first of these someone came and gave her a paper having words of Hebrew on it. She complained to the presence in the dream that she did not know Hebrew. Then the voice said: "That which is written commands you to return to Israel."

Two months later, in a second dream, a man told her: "In the same way as God told Abraham: 'You are going into Canaan,' so I tell you that you are going into the land of Israel."

In another dream, she was reading the 83rd Psalm which was being shown her by a Catholic priest. The words she read (which she showed me now in her Italian bible) were:

"They have said, Come, and let us cut them off from being a nation; that the name of Israel may be no more in remembrance."

In the dream following after this, a child took her by the hand and said: "You know that your Kibbutz is going to another place."

At this time, she did not know what the word *Kibbutz* meant, until on waking she got in touch with some Jews, who explained its meaning to her.

By now the events in Garganico were beginning to attract wide attention. Two journalists came from Rome and photographed the villagers. A representative of the American Joint Distribution Committee arrived next, and told them how to get to Israel.

At this time, half of those men who had been converted were circumcised, the others not. She was told in a dream now that every man who wanted to go to Israel must be circumcised. (She heard only a voice in this dream, and saw no one.)

The prospective immigrants went to Rome and those who

had not been, were circumcised. The news of this made headlines in the Italian Press.

Signora Bonfitto's narrative ended here—a little abruptly,
perhaps. We all stood up, and she waited in the background,
with an expression on her face of having switched off her
attention. The others brought out copies of the Italian news-
papers and showed me the rather ribald headlines, of which the
following is a sample: "The Last Six of their Males Circumcised, the Villagers of Garganico Depart for Israel." There
were also some rather sensational photographs of the group
standing round Signora Bonfitto whose head was gazing sky-
wards, her hands uplifted, and her mouth opened as though to
let out a prophetic cry. It looked like a religious meeting of
negroes in Alabama.

The converts seemed to take all this without either annoyance
or any sense of humour. They were modest but proud of it as
a tribute to the state of grace in which they lived. Their publicity—they seemed to think—witnessed to the light that shone
forth from Garganico.

"And you actually still have some paper left in your notebook?" laughed David, as I returned it to my pocket.

We went out of doors and I took a photograph of the Italians,
standing in their fields with Mount Hermon in the distance
behind them. It was sunset and on these uplands I saw that
mysterious Biblical light which shows when the rays of a rising
moon cross those of a setting sun, and every blade of grass is
moonlit-blue on one side, sunset-gold on the other.

As we departed in the car, with a Tunisian who wanted a lift
settled in the back, David stood waving to us in the fields,
against a green background, like a fairy figure drawn round the
word *Finis* at the end of a tale.

But there was a postscript. The Tunisian started talking
about his neighbours, the twelve Italian families. "They refuse
to cultivate their fields this year," he said, "they say it is the
Seventh year, the Sabattical year, when the Mosaic Law tells

them not to do so. The Rabbi comes along and says they must, because the government wants them to grow food, but they say they know better. They read what to do and what not to do in the Bible and take no notice of whomever tells them differently."

CHAPTER XI

LIFE IN THE KIBBUTZIM

IN some ways, the most exciting, stimulating and successful development in all Israel is the collective agricultural settlements, the *Kibbutzim*.

The history of these settlements goes back to long before the founding of the Jewish state, to the proposals for colonizing Palestine, which were discussed at the Second Zionist Congress held at Basel in August 1898, when a Colonization Fund was set up.

The idea of colonization was that the Jewish communities should be agricultural settlements. The socialists already had become an influential group among the Zionists. And the pogroms in Russia in 1903, together with the failure of the Russian Revolution of 1905, led to an extensive immigration into Palestine of Russian socialist Jews, with all the ideas and ideals of that phase of the Russian Revolution.

These were the real founders of the Settlements, and some of the Kibbutzim—places like the large and successful Kibbutz Afikim with its 2,000 settlers, and its successful ply-wood industry—this influence is still predominant. In Afikim they have printed and published in the Kibbutz itself the history of the settlement. It is most interesting to compare the look of some of the older members, with their contented faces, egg-shaped and bald except for the cauliflower-textured hair at the sides of their heads—with the photographs of the handsome burning-eyed revolutionaries they were when they came out of Russia and started this settlement on the treeless soil. The anarchist-revolutionaries of to-day look thoroughly bourgeois at Afikim, where they are building small two-storied houses in which they collect their belongings and live a life of well-deserved comfort, undisturbed by the challenge of ideas from the outside world. They have even introduced that most counter-revolutionary of symbols in the Kibbutz—the indoor separate lavatory and washroom with shower—into Afikim.

All the same it is well to remember that the Russian or Polish immigrant, fleeing from the suppression of a revolution early in this century, is the dominating governmental type in Israel—the type of Ben Gurion himself.

My friend Isaiah Berlin has suggested to me that the key to understanding Israel is to realize that its ideals came out of the Liberal and Socialist revolutionary movements of Russia at the beginning of this century. For this reason—he says—there is something misleading about comparing the socialism of Mapai with the British Labour Party, or Mapam with the communist parties of to-day. His line of argument suggests that —paradoxically—there may be something of anachronism about the political ideas of the new State, or at least about the background of intellectual life out of which these ideas are born. This would certainly explain the air of unassailable complacency which one finds in a place like Afikim where those ideas have worked out very well for the settlement itself, as also the lack of reality among the followers of Mapam, especially in their attitude to Russia—which perhaps they think of as the Russia of 1905.

The idea of the Kibbutz was a kind of communist anarchism. The communities were in the beginning literally and rigidly communist in practising a complete equality. They were far more communist than Karl Marx: in fact they were as communist as the monasteries of primitive Christianity, or as the theories of Tolstoi.

A monastic communism was achieved by removing money and all personal property from the use of individuals. All property was communal. In the early, now almost "classical" days of the Kibbutz, even clothes were regarded only as being loaned to the wearer during the days that they were actually on his or her body. Sent to the Kibbutz laundry, they automatically became the community's property again and would be re-issued to anyone else whom they happened approximately to fit.

In these early days there was almost no privacy. The cultural and family life of the Kibbutz were enjoyed in the evening get-togethers with guitars, singing and discussion.

Individualism of a kind which nourished on solitude was discouraged, and perhaps even impossible. Women were not supposed to seek to make themselves attractive by dress and adornment. In principle they shared all the tasks of the community equally with men. If, in the long run, it was more practicable for them to do the household tasks of the community—such as work in kitchen and laundry—than work in the fields, this was not a matter of principle but simply a question of someone having to do these things for which women happen to be well adapted, but which were regarded as the equals of the other tasks. In principle, they might equally well have been working in the fields, as in fact those who were freed from the general domesticity did do.

To-day the Kibbutzim present a very different picture from those early pioneering communities. This is partly the result of the inevitable tendency of such organizations to develop away from abstract principles towards those arrangements which have worked out best in practice. For example, the principle of everyone sharing clothes which belonged to the whole community did not work out well in practice. Nature has not made us all egalitarian in the shape and size of our bodies. This already introduces a principle of selective distribution among us; people were found (if it was necessary to discover such a thing) to take better care of their own clothes than of those belonging to everyone.

Out of the absurdity of sharing clothes the Kibbutzim have

developed an efficient way of looking after the clothes of members. Everyone's clothes are numbered, and next to the laundry there is a locker bearing this number. You hand in your clothes to the wash and later they turn up automatically in your numbered locker.

Improvements in the rooms which members are allotted have also led to the development of greater individualism. Paradoxically, the wireless — generally regarded as a great leveller — has had the same result. For to-day people tend after meals to drift back to their rooms in order to listen to a programme.

Moreover, the accumulation of communal property tends to result in its becoming, in all but name, private property. The community buys books. These books are found in the rooms of those who care to read them—and of these the teachers have the prime claim. It buys reproductions of paintings; and the same thing happens. Nor is furniture suddenly withdrawn from the use of members.

Privileges also grow up. The Kibbutz builds a new and better type of dwellings. Inevitably and rightly, there are members of the Kibbutz who have a claim on these which is superior to other claims.

In Afikim there is a painter who lives in the Kibbutz. He has a studio which has been specially built for him by the community, and recently he was sent to France and Italy in order to study.

His main effort is painting murals for the large communal eating room, to illustrate the significance of festivals celebrated by the Kibbutz. He also paints easel paintings, and Kibbutz members are able to choose what they want from these and hang them in their rooms.

He is a German painter, and he described to me how his whole conception of style had changed from the ideas of German expressionism to something quite different as the result of his being a member of the Kibbutz. It was not exactly that the needs of the members of the Kibbutz to have the symbols of their festivities expressed for them in his paintings had become the goal of his own work. Rather, it was his ambition to give form in his own way to the vague imaginings of the other Kibbutz members who looked to him to shape their ideas.

From seeing his paintings I could see that he was more interested to-day in painting large murals than in doing smaller canvases. However, as often happens when artists seek to serve the community, it strikes the spectator who sees the results that they have merely reduced the quantity of their imagination and the quality of their work in order to produce what they think the community wants; and in their work they reveal their secret opinion that the community's standards are not only different but worse than their own.

It is possible that, to-day, an artist of authentic gifts could not compromise with the community, or with his own ideas of the community. Perhaps the attempt to do so always indicates some degree of failure of personality. On the other hand, it is possible that an artist who painted for the community in the sense of realizing ideas which were his own personal experience of socialism, might create something at once completely un-compromising and capable of expressing those ideas in their intrinsic goodness which nearly always become debased when they are adapted to needs of communal living or political needs. A great social art might be created by someone caring deeply about society if he were determined never to meet the community half-way, and was contemptuous of the day-to-day policy of the committees directing the community.

At present the Kibbutz seems to be at the stage when artists and writers there are concerned with using their talents to absorb and transmit its rather puritan ethics. *Zionist Newsletter* (Vol. IV, No. 19, July 8th, 1952) summarizes the plot of a short story by Nathan Shacham, called *Inside the Room*. This story appeared in the literary periodical called *Orlogin*. The summary and extracts are so revealing both of the Kibbutzim and of the attitude of an Israeli writer, that it is worth quoting:

"Nathan Shacham's story . . . is a study of the psychology of a man who does not quite fit into the Kibbutz framework. The hero has been falling down on his job, and is deeply disturbed at the suggestion that he should hand it over to one of the younger generation who is better fitted for it. It is only the love and sympathy of his wife that bring him ultimately to the realization that there are more important things in life, and especially in the Kibbutz, than personal prestige and honour.

" 'She loves me', he thinks, 'although I am not the finest kind of person, because I am the father of her children, she has attained what I have been unable to attain. She has liberated herself from the desire to reach the "top of the tree", to be the strongest, to be the focal point. She accepts her fate with a clear mind, and she needs no illusions. She has absorbed in her blood the ideal of "equality of benefits", without continuing to nourish false dreams in the recesses of her soul. "We live too close together, and there is no room for lies amongst us . . ." ' he remembered her words.

"He continued to think of her with appreciation. 'I have a wife who lives by concepts which I have not yet succeeded in absorbing. She belongs to the future and I belong to the past'. She lay in his bed and personified at the same time both home and the outside world. Within his walls she demanded that he should take responsibility, and took her place on the side of society's judgment against him. She was the Kibbutz within his room. She caused him pain, and he loved her."

It is strange to think that, in a rather different form, this story is a parable which would be accepted in a very large part of the world to-day. The Kibbutz in your bed is not so very different from the Russian or the Chinese dictator's photograph over your bed, so far as the moral that the social conscience interpreted in terms of everyone fitting in with the groups or the community's immediate needs, is concerned. Of course, there is the great difference that in Israel to be or not to be a member of the Kibbutz is a purely voluntary decision; and yet to be a member produces this attitude, and, indeed, it is difficult to think of any other ethic which the Kibbutz could have. For if the moral of the story had been that the man was justified in being a misfit, and the wife wrong in bringing the Kibbutz into their marriage bed, then they would have had to leave the Kibbutz anyway.

However, to return to the subject of the painter at Afikim. His development and his attitude are significant of a change in the attitude of the Kibbutz to the individual. First, his individual needs—studio, canvases, paints, etc.—are property which, although technically not belonging to him, could be of no use to anyone else in the community. Secondly, his products, although primarily for the community dining hall, can also be in the rooms of the Kibbutniks. Thirdly, he is sent abroad and given privileges other Kibbutniks do not have, because it is felt that everyone will benefit from his advantages.

That women are able to dress more individually, that there is more privacy and so on are also benefits which indirectly benefit all. They are, therefore, natural and commonsensical.

On the other hand, the prosperity of a place like Afikim had its depressing side. Here in a very large settlement, people were developing home lives and forming little groups of friends who dropped in on one another and there seemed to be a good many people whose circle shut them off from the rest of the Kibbutz though they had no window open on to the outside world. The effort to know everybody and widen the consciousness of each individual to include the community had been dropped, and at the same time the cliques which had been formed among families and friends were too small. The general result of this seemed to be a kind of pervasive boredom and an acceptance of second-rate standards. The rooms in the comfortable new Kibbutz buildings, with their minuscule reproductions of Modiglianis and flower pieces by Van Gogh on the walls, seemed characteristic. It was a doll's house world in which civilization had shrunk.

Perhaps—if my impressions are at all justified—the reason

is that Afikim is too large for such a type of community. The question of how large a community of people trying to lead the life of the Kibbutz should be, is obviously a very relevant one. For if the community be too small, it is little more than a family, like a farmer's household. But if it be too large, it tends to break up into small groups. As it prospers it becomes simply an association of people benefiting materially from the results of a certain system of joint enterprise which no longer challenges them in a way to produce a positive communal spirit.

There must clearly be an ideal number for such a community: that is, if one is not thinking of it simply as an agricultural or industrial enterprise, but as a way of life producing a certain culture of its own.

The ideal number of members would seem to be between two and three hundred, and not more than five hundred. Within such limits every member can contain within his single consciousness the consciousness of all, whilst at the same time the personal qualities of each one are diffused among all.

The so-called Crisis of the Kibbutz is another cause which pushes forward the development of the Kibbutzim.

This crisis is caused by a variety of things. One is the inflation which has upset the economy of the whole country. Many of the settlements are heavily indebted, or are unable to raise funds for capital projects. In a brilliantly informative article in *The New Yorker*, John Hersey describes the measures some Kibbutzim are forced to use to keep financially afloat. He gives a picture of secretaries of the communal committees rushing from one bank to another in an endeavour to obtain cash by giving a cheque to the first bank which is drawn on an account at the second and then having to give the second one a cheque drawn on supposed funds at a third, and then the third a cheque on a fourth account, and so on, in an unfortunately not unending series; but they hope that before their total lack of funds will be discovered money will somehow have come in from someone or somewhere.

Hersey describes a meeting at a fundless Kibbutz where everyone agreed that the last money should be spent in obtaining a jeep for the secretary, to be used for this purpose.

Even if things are not everywhere quite so desperate and so farcical as this, the financial crisis is certainly a very grave aspect of the general one. But the worst perhaps lies in the attitude of the new immigrants to the Kibbutzim.

These immigrants have flooded into the towns. They prefer the free-enterprise and black market of the ma'bara to going on to the land and renouncing personal gain and property.

The result of their indifference has been that the percentage of the Kibbutz population to that of the rest of Israel has sunk from six to four per cent. This means a consequent drop in the prestige of the Kibbutzim. The Kibbutz always represented a small minority, but formally this was an effective one. Now it risks becoming ineffective.

Instead of being the pioneers the "chosen few" who are at the head of a movement whose influence is felt by all instead of being the fountain of purest Zionism poured over the land of the Ingathering and making it to flower, the Kibbutz population suddenly appears a monastic cult of specialists who have chosen to lead this particular kind of life.

Apart from the indifference of the immigrants, the political split between the Mapai and Mapam, in addition to splitting up some of the communal settlements, has caused a good many people to leave them altogether.

Often now you hear people reflect that the task of the Kibbutzim may after all have been fulfilled. They suggest that some pattern of living on the countryside which is different from the present one, while perhaps growing out of it, should be evolved. The Kibbutzim must be transformed if they are to survive.

All the same, the visits I made to Kibbutzim persuaded me

that these settlements still have much of great importance to
offer Israel.

There is a tendency to regard the pattern of the Kibbutz as
the same everywhere. But actually I found that the settlements
differ greatly from one another, with a different atmosphere
in each group, very different buildings and surroundings even,
different politics and beliefs. The principles of the Kibbutz
movement—working on the land and sharing benefits—remain the same but they are capable of great variety of inter-
pretation.

In a previous chapter, I noted the attitude of the educator
I met towards the policy of separating parents from their
children, of which he thoroughly approved. But at Sde Eliahu,
an orthodox Kibbutz which I visited later, houses were being
built with a room between the rooms of two married couples in
which the children of both families could sleep. In making this
experiment, the orthodox may, despite their conservatism, be
more advanced than the Mapam; and some non-orthodox
communities are moving in the same direction.

In the beautiful hills of Ephraim, there is the Kibbutz
Hazorea, looking across a wide valley to the mountains, one of
which is Mount Tabor: a green mountain separate from the
rest, with up-springing butting shape, which leapt into my
mind like those biblical hills "leaping like rams," and bringing
with it also thoughts of Milton. The evening when I arrived
at Hazorea was exceptionally beautiful, cool and full of relief
with a change of wind which ended five days of Khamsin, when
the hot wind blew across the desert to Israel, and the weather
was transported out of July into April. There were long
shadows and the valley was golden-green with an exhalation
of silver dust, a thin veil in front of the mountains.

Kibbutz Hazorea, a very successful centre for agriculture, is
also a shrine for Wilfrid Israel, the English-born Jew of a
Berlin family who was killed when the aeroplane in which he

was flying to Lisbon—Leslie Howard was also among the
passengers—was shot down by the Germans. A temple-like
building encloses the Wilfrid Israel museum—the collection
which he chose with the purpose of illustrating in examples of
early art the inter-connectedness of Western and Eastern influences, the Greek with the Asian.

The Wilfrid Israel building also includes a reading room,
decorated with one of those modernist decorations by an
Israeli artist which doesn't by any means come off—and an
open air theatre. Some of the leading members of the Kibbutz
were friends of Wilfrid Israel who, although he never took the
final step of living in Israel, seems to have left his heart in this
place. There is no doubt that this memorial to a sensitive,
highly-cultivated and rather unhappy man, killed before he
had achieved what might well have been a great life's work,
gives Kibbutz Hazorea a feeling of spiritual dedication to high
personal values which is rare.

How different from this though is the atmosphere of Kfar
Hanassi in the Upper Galilee, to which I went immediately
after two days at Hazorea. This is not far from Alma, the village
of the Italian Jews, and has a similar view, with waving fields of
barley at the edge of the high plateau above the Jordan valley.
There is a wonderful view up the valley to the north, with the
beautiful white sign of Mount Hermon in the sky, and below its
foot-hills Lake Hula, spreading rather untidily in the flat
valley, a formless relative of the beautifully ovaloid Lake of
Tiberias to the south. Across the Jordan I saw once more the
line of Transjordan mountains, flowing against the sky like a
river placed sideways.

Kfar Hanassi is a pioneer Kibbutz still in the exciting
phase of being created. A few hut-like houses are spread out at
the edge of the fields on a green out of which there sprout
the tender shoots of pine and larch which in twenty years will
make this a gracious place of shadow and greenery even in the
height of the summer.

At Kfar Hanassi there are a good many Jews who have come from England. The secretary, called Michael, is the son of a rabbi, and comes from Glasgow. It was strange to me to hear him talking in his strong Glasgow dialect about his youth as a Scottish Jew. Michael told me that when he was a student he already had the idea of going to a Kibbutz and had received his training in England.

Many of the Kibbutzim, in addition to agriculture, have some small industry attached to them. In Kfar Hanassi, this is making the bronze joints of pipes, which are cast in moulds.

In the centre of the Kibbutz there is a building in construction —either for hall or school rooms, I forget which. The reason why it has not been finished is characteristic of the present economic condition of Israel. When money was received for it from abroad, the secretariat of the Kibbutz changed it into Israeli money: but, having done this, the cost of the materials was already much greater than it had been when the estimate was made for the building and the money obtained. Thus the Kibbutz has only been able to obtain part of the necessary material and the building is left unfinished. Michael told me this sadly. I reflected that there must be many projects in Israel abandoned for the same reason.

Of all the places I went to, the most congenial to me were Kfar Hanassi and Neoth Mordechai, still further North in Galilee.

Neoth Mordechai is in the fantastically fertile valley of the Upper Jordan, which runs along the northernmost edge of the Kibbutz. The soil is loamy and black. In the course of a few years the members have been very successful in growing a great variety of fruit trees and crops here. There are also cattle and artificial ponds for intensified breeding of fish. The local industry—as usual in the Kibbutzim due to the special ingeniousness of one member who developed this as a side-line— is a factory for making shoes.

The inhabitants of Neoth Mordechai are very mixed. They include many different kinds of Europeans, Africans and Asiatics among whom are Cochin Indian Jews—rather rare specimens, even for Israel. The Kibbutz is non-party and is distinguished by an air of tolerance and kindness which is most impressive.

A leading spirit of Neoth Mordechai is a young man, approaching middle-age, called Balu. Balu is from Germany, and if I had met him anywhere except in the Kibbutz I would have put him down as a dreamy, sensitive, perhaps rather melancholic type of German Jew: not, indeed, altogether unlike Wilfrid Israel, whom I had known in Berlin, and who—perhaps because he never decided to live in the Kibbutz Hazorea which he so loved appeared to spend his whole life wandering along the margin of some great action.

But at Neoth Mordechai the dreaminess of such a person becomes the imaginative sympathy which includes within one mind all the activities of the Kibbutz. His intellectual superiority has widened and deepened instead of remaining above and outside the efforts of those who are less intelligent. When Balu showed me round the orchards, the cornfields, the fish-ponds and the shoe factory, I had the sense of the energetic personal feeling which had gone into these things.

All the same, he was conscious enough of failures and defects. The fruit trees, for example, had been planted too close together, because in that way they grew quickly and competitively and produced fruit sooner. Here—as everywhere in Israel, the young country in a hurry—they had to go in for quick results. But one of these results was to exhaust the soil so that the trees would have to be torn up and new ones planted in a few years time.

Then he spoke of the locusts which just at this time were reported as being across the Jordan border, and which threatened to come this way at any moment, and he told me about the fires which several times had destroyed their crops two years in succession. He spoke also about the khamsin, of which I had had six days: the wind blowing across the Sahara desert, which is supposed to blow for fifty—khamsin means fifty—days of every year in Israel. "When I first came here I hardly noticed it. People complained about the khamsin, and I wondered what they were talking about. My second year, I began to feel it as a nuisance. By my third year I had come to dread it. And now it seems to me almost more than I can stand."

He used almost exactly the same words as I had heard from others in Jerusalem and Tel-Aviv. Locusts, fire and khamsin. For Europeans there are some aspects of life in the Middle East which they can never quite accept or get used to and which therefore, with time, become more and more discouraging. The European accepts the idea of work, however hard and difficult it may be. He does not accept the idea of overwhelming fatalities of nature which make his work completely wasted. He expects too to be able to retain his faith in his own work. Forces which repeatedly gnaw away, undermine and destroy all his efforts—like ants eating up the whole of literature—seem outside civilization. They eat up the inside of the brain, excoriate the nerves, become a kind of palpable omnipresent force of despair which the Easterner can perhaps accept fatalistically, but which the Westerner knows less and less how to deal with in a country like Israel, the longer he stays.

Then—Balu went on—there was the question of sanitation. Had I noticed this? Indeed I had. The lavatories at Neoth Mordechai (as at several other Kibbutzim I had visited) consisted of wooden sheds placed over open pits. When one pit was filled, another was dug, the shed moved over it and the previous pit filled in. These methods did not prevent the smell being noticeable throughout a great deal of the settlement, even in the not too warm weather.

In the early days it was rather a matter of pride for us of the Kibbutzim, Balu explained, to be indifferent to the niceties of sanitation. Such a contempt, for the pruderies, intimacies and decencies, somehow emphasized more than anything else their superiority to mere material considerations. It had also something about it of defiant puritanism, I suppose, of vigorous demonstration that to the pure all things are pure.

All the same, Balu went on to say, perhaps this policy had been mistaken because it had involved putting what should have been the first things last. To-day it would cost many times more to put in proper sanitation than it would have done at the beginning. Prices had increased enormously, and besides this it would be far more difficult to lay the pipes, now that the buildings of the settlement had been completed. But when they started, they had other things to pay for and construct: the power plant, the first tractors, the observation tower and other urgent military arrangements for protecting a camp which was almost on the frontier.

In a community of this size, it was possible for a man like Balu, without his having to become a politician, without any excessive toughening of his character, and without his having to conceal his misgivings about certain things, to become a leader of the Kibbutz. Talking with him, I felt that the anarchism of the Kibbutzim should not be lost. It provides the example of a kind of leadership of men who have not lost contact with their own personalities, which the world greatly needs.

At Neoth Mordechai there was a high degree of what the outside world would consider standards of civilization. The members enjoyed a considerable amount of privacy, they had a few possessions of their own, and they even indulged in a certain amount of entertainment of their friends in their rooms.

Among the friends I made there, were an American scientist called Herman, and his wife. Herman had thrown up his job in America in order to come and do agriculture on the Kibbutz. There was also a Czech, Peter, and his German wife, Frieda. Peter was sympathetic to the politics of Mapam, though not quite convinced by them. He was one of those for whom dislike of America has become a bug which affects their view of anything. An interesting debate between the East and West was going on in his mind; and characteristically, the same arguments which he used to condemn the lack of "real freedom," and the witch-hunting in America, were used to excuse and justify these very things in Eastern Europe. With a person like him who excuses lack of freedom in Russia by condemning it in America, perhaps really we are up against the scruple of conscience which makes some people condemn faults in those they love with such virulence that they excuse the same faults in those they hate.

His wife, Frieda, however did not at all share his views when she detected him using dishonest arguments which were the perverse results of his own fearlessness and integrity. She had the still greater honesty which comes not just out of a tormented conscience but out of the warmth of feeling of the heart. Perhaps also the simple fact that she and her husband were living in Israel and not in Czecho-Slovakia made her think that they had made a choice which they could not go back on by abstract argumentation.

Balu, Herman and Peter, were people of such fine intelligence that they suggested another problem of the Kibbutz. Is a young scientist with the devotion and capacity of Herman being of as much use to Israel in the kibbutz as he might be in a laboratory or a factory? The idea that he was romantically wasting his time had occurred to others, and pressure had been brought on him to go back to America for a while and receive the best possible technical training. He had refused to do so, and if there is certainly an element of waste in his resistance, the good that is done to a country by people being allowed to choose to do what they want, is among the impalpables which may be found to have more value than the directors of labour in other countries realize to-day. At any rate, the Kibbutz system depends on people going there who are in a sense above the provincialism, and cleverer than the technical requirements of such communities. It is the superior qualities of people like Balu and Herman which give a Kibbutz like Neoth Mordechai its peculiar elatedness and sense of direction.

In Neoth Mordechai, the increase of individual means of self-expression, had not led to the fragmentation of the life of the community, which was too small to be broken up in this way.

Although people who received, for example, food parcels from abroad (these were rather frowned on in the Kibbutz) or who had books and wireless sets of their own, lived slightly better than their neighbours during their leisure hours, this did not matter, because all these things were known and understood by their fellow-members, to some extent shared by all, and in any case rapidly expendable.

The really basic thing is that no one had money. This struck me more and more as the key fact about the Kibbutzim—that they were co-operatives of people who had agreed to produce and sell goods jointly, sharing the benefits received in the form of goods and not as money.

That they received goods which can be valued in terms of money and that they belonged to an organization actually selling and buying things with money, seems to me irrelevant. The point is that they had cut out of their lives the whole complex which makes people in modern society think that money represents freedom, because they can make more and more of it, buying security, leisure and entertainments; only to discover that it also represents slavery, since it condemns them to work harder and harder to gain the abstract currency which is then taken away in the form of taxation before they can concretize it into any of these solid benefits.

The Kibbutznik has ceased to bother about all this. He has simply ceased to think about earning and spending at all. All he asks is to be provided with the simple goods—roof, food, a few bare necessities and a few possibilities of amusement— which add up to no more than the necessities of living and

L

working, combined with the amenities of the whole community.

From the point of view of the individual member, much of the attraction of the Kibbutz seems to me this operation which has been performed on the function of money in his life.

Outside the Kibbutz, even the bare apparatus of living has to be earned, unless one lives on a dole, which is also money. For people to-day do not just work and earn: they live in a very complicated sum of what is being given to them and what taken away, which they are expected to understand, and which at the best is difficult and confusing. To put it at its worst, it has complicated life to such an extent that to-day in most countries it is probably having a profound effect on our characters. People no longer think even in terms of the getting and spending which Wordsworth deplored in his famous sonnet. They think in terms of adapting themselves to an immense economic spider's web in which they are caught up: where certain things are automatically provided for them by society; certain things gained by their own efforts; and certain things then taken away. And all this is worked out in terms of money, earning, spending, benefits, and taxation. Everyone is expected first and foremost, and will be expected more and more, to be primarily a business man, making his calculations—that before everything else. Freedom from confusion and worries can only be obtained by skill in business; because the business man is the one who can immediately trace his position on the chart of public economy, and who therefore knows where he is and what he can do.

Simplicity of living has been completely abolished by systems which make everyone's status a ratio between their own and the State's calculations about their economic situation on the chart. For simplicity depends on being able to live on your own minimal earnings with such small claims being made by you and on you, that you are independent of economic calculations.

When one considers the effect that dependence on usury is supposed to have had on the Jewish character one wonders what the modern universal awareness that everyone is an "economic unit" is going to have on future generations. The Jews, being cut off from making things and from creating, and entirely dependent on doing dealings with money, are supposed to have become very abstract-minded. This supposedly explains the lack of concreteness of the Jewish character—the love of theories and abstractions, the tendencies to make vast, yet meticulously worked-out generalizing theories about society, the lack of concrete grasp of single instances.

It is likely that the modern tendency to make everyone think of himself as an economic unit moving from a socially insured cradle to a socially insured grave, will emphasize the mental dependence of individuals on their crudely solid evaluation by values which become increasingly simple money values. The individualist will become simply the social misfit, and individual values only accepted in so far as they are money values.

The Kibbutz is interesting and important because it shows us how a socialist community can overcome the worst danger of socialism—this converting of everyone into a money-symbol—by simply cutting money out of personal lives altogether. Whether such an experiment, though successful sometimes in a small community, could be adapted to a whole society, is doubtful; and as we have seen, the Kibbutz has its own way of undermining individual values. All the same, such an experiment is particularly interesting to-day when the whole world—whatever its politics—is moving increasingly towards socialist solutions of every economic problem.

Could the economy of a whole country—say a country like England—be organized on the lines of a Kibbutz? This would mean that the State, instead of being a tax receiver, would be the chief handler of money in the community. Like the secretariat of the Kibbutz it would sell goods to other countries, and buy imports which it would then distribute among the community. The population would be rich or poor not in money but in actual things, which would be distributed according to the community's prosperity, and with regard to individual needs. There would be no taxation, because the State itself would have the money which it now, by an incredibly elaborate procedure, takes away from those who have earned it.

Of course, just to put forward such an idea is to reveal its glaring flaw. The success of the Kibbutz depends on its being a small community in which everyone knows everyone else in a personal way, and in which social justice is built not on official-dom but on friendship.

Sometimes though it is worth putting an absurdity forward not only just to show it is absurd, but to show that something else is very unsatisfactory also. And the picture I have just drawn, though impossible to realize, does have this effect of criticizing the way in which we live in modern societies where a collective economic system has been worked out which bat-tens on the fruits of an outmoded individualist economy: with the result that the individual has become a function motivated by the old incentives which he then has to adapt to the new system.

The Kibbutz then, although going through its "crisis", is a subject of perennial interest—and has been ever since people thought of forming small ideal communities to get away from the social system. That it has been successful, and that the Israeli social system is now perhaps moving away from it, make it all the more interesting. There is more than pathos, too, in the fact that the towns and the black market in a country which can offer no one economic security should be destroy-ing it.

One of its most striking successes has been in the handling of cases of individual hardship. Each Kibbutz is run by a committee, elected annually, which meets the whole community at weekly or monthly intervals. At such meetings, the work programme of members is discussed and decided on, and fur-ther decisions about how to spend the resources of the com-munity are made.

I have already quoted the example of Kibbutz Afikim sending their painter Kibbutznik to Italy and France: a major economic decision for them to have taken in the present situation, by the way. This is though only one example of the consideration shown by the Kibbutzim to the individual case. The sick are sent abroad—to America, for example—to the greatest specialists in their illnesses. One such case struck me particularly. A member of one Kibbutz had an accident in which he lost the use of his hands and feet. Being a very active man, he was suicidally depressed by his disability. His fellow Kibbutzniks found a man from another settlement who was also completely incapacitated. They arranged for the two to meet in order that the one who had been helpless for many years should explain to their comrade how he had been able to enjoy life in some ways despite his disadvantages. Then they studied ways of arranging the Kibbutznik's room so that he could do as many things as possible unaided: for instance, turn on taps and the light with the stumps of his hands.

While I was at Neoth Mordechai there was Passover.

"And it shall be when thy son asketh thee in time to come, saying What is this? that thou shalt say unto him, By strength of hand the Lord brought us out of Egypt, from the house of bondage."

The Passover is the celebration of the journey of the Children of Israel from Egypt to Canaan, under the leadership of Moses. The festival is devoted primarily to instructing the children how these things happened.

So the children are taken into the fields and made to witness the blessing and the dedication of the crops. And in the evening, after the Passover Feast—the one meal in Israel to-day where large quantities of meat are consumed—the children are made to ask: "What is the difference between this night and other nights?" And the answer comes: "This night we eat *matza* and no leavened bread."

"We shall now tell the story of how we came out of Egypt," the recitation of the ceremony begins.

"To-night let everyone who is hungry eat with us."

"This year we are slaves in Egypt but next year we shall be free."

And so on.

Before this there had been the ceremony in the fields, when all the children of the Kibbutz were crowded with their parents into lorries and at sunset were driven out into the fields of high corn.

Then the feast of the whole Kibbutz and of many visitors, held in a hall on the outskirts of the settlement, because there were too many for the dining room.

We all crowded on to narrow planks placed across packing cases to serve as benches; Peter put more meat on to his plate than I have ever seen any one consume in one meal before. A sweetish wine was served in cups, and *matza* was eaten with the meat.

The engineer whom I had seen in the morning working his lathe in the tool shop of the Kibbutz was now the conductor of the orchestra and of a choir consisting of children from the settlement. They performed the cantata, which consisted partly of traditional, partly of modern songs to illustrate the story of the Passover. The singing was very beautiful.

Coming out of the Diaspora and entering into the Promised Land has the greatest significance for people in Israel to-day. No one can attend the Passover without feeling that it applies as much to themselves as to the followers of Moses. It is inevitably a feast which has the deepest significance for both orthodox and unorthodox. It is not only the celebration of a past religious experience but participation in the miracle of our own times.

Some of the unorthodox have tried to rewrite and recreate the Passover ceremony, giving it words and music adapted to recent events, even to the story of their own Kibbutz.

It will be interesting to see whether a new development in
Hebrew literature may not grow out of these anonymous efforts
of the Kibbutzim. One rather fears not, because, as I have pointed
out, the Kibbutz seems scarcely a fostering ground for genius.
Yet a development of the Hebrew religion along these lines is
perhaps possible for the reason that although the writers be
agnostic, the religious overtones of the Passover are unavoidable. However agnostic its words the ceremony cannot avoid
identifying Jewish history of to-day with the deliverance of
Moses. The Jews of this generation live in a time when the
past has been fulfilled and the present transformed. Perhaps
the endeavour of the irreligious and unorthodox to create a new
myth out of this, might be the very means by which the old
religion was reborn. There is certainly exactly the same need
to tell the children about 1948 as there was to tell them about
the crossing of the Red Sea when the waters were pushed back.
To tell the story memorably though, a great religious poetry is
necessary.

CHAPTER XII

JEWS OF COCHIN,
SEPHARDIM AND YEMENITES

AMONG the inhabitants of Neoth Mordechai, some of the most interesting are a group of Cochin Jews, from India.

The Cochin Jews are perhaps the least Jewish-looking Jews (according to my own idea of what Jews should look like) even in Israel where most people look unexpected. They resemble Malayans or Chinese rather than Jews, with their broad foreheads, high mongolian cheekbones, narrow, almond-shaped rather blood-shot eyes, squat noses, and thick lips. Their skin is of a varnished, golden-brown colour, and they have straight, black hair.

In an article in *Zion**, Dr. J. Vainstein writes of the Jews of Cochin that they "reside in the south-east corner of India, by the shores of the Indian Ocean," and that they certainly constitute one of the most ancient Jewish communities:

"Jews have lived here uninterruptedly for at least 1600 years. There are among the Cochin Jews who relate that ships of King Solomon's fleet visited the ports of Quilon and Cottayam. Others believe that they are descendants of the lost ten tribes brought there by Salmanassar, King of Assyria; still others maintain that their forefathers came to the port of Malabar, Cranganore, on the Malabar coast, after the destruction of the First Temple. All of them, however, are quite certain that they came to these shores not later than after the destruction of the Second Temple."

They are, therefore, like the Yemenites, one of the Jewish

Zion, Volume II, No. 3-4.

communities whose origins are hidden in the deepest obscurity. Like the Yemenites also, they have about them a kind of untouched purity.

In India, they suffered from no persecution. On the contrary they were regarded as a caste with considerable privileges. Their reasons for coming to Israel are therefore purely religious. As Dr. Vainstein, who has visited this community in India, reports:

> "In the establishment of the State of Israel the Cochin Jews see the fulfilment of the Divine Promise; they have a burning desire for Aliyah which finds expression in their continuous and increasing pressure for immigration."

I was extremely interested in meeting some Cochin Jews. Fortunately my friends at Neoth Mordechai were on excellent terms with a group of them, and a meeting was easily arranged. As a group they were shy—especially the women—but one of them, called David, talked freely when we were alone together.

David spoke English quite well, with a slow, sweet, almost singing intonation. What he said was obviously the result of careful thinking on the subject, and I was struck by his reasonableness and his spontaneous, willing nature.

In Cochin—he told me—he had been a clerk. He had earned good money, and was better fed and clothed than he could hope to be in Israel.

"Why then did you come here?"

"Oh, that was the result of our religion. You see, it was our belief that whenever it became possible we Cochin Indians should return to the home we had come from many hundreds of years ago."

He talked about his religion of the Ingathering not as though it were something invisible like a belief, but as though it were solid and real as the ship that brought them to the shores of Israel—as though the Cochin Indians had had their tickets to Palestine for 2,000 years, and were only waiting for the date to

be announced when they would use them. And of course when
the ship arrived they would only have feelings of joy to step on
board it.

"Now you are here are you glad you came?"

"Well, yes, I am glad." He said in his heavy, sweet, ponder-
ing way. "On the whole I am glad. We do not have so much to
eat, and we have to work harder. But all this was explained to
us before we came, and we quite understood how it would be.
I must say that here too we are more looked after. When we
were there, although we had good work, our employers were
not interested in caring for us: the future was uncertain.
People here are really interested in us, we feel. I must say that.
Here we feel that we are cared for."

"Then it's all just as you expected?"

"Oh yes. It was explained to us that life would be hard. And
it is hard. We expected that and we are quite happy about it."

This was a different attitude from that of the Moroccans.
It had the noble simplicity of an uncontaminated people.

The Indian children whom I met in the Mapai Kibbutz of
Gal-Ed, were very different from this.

In the first place, they were members of the Sephardi Community of Indian Jews who are, by origin, Iraqis. The great
grandparents of these children were from those Jews who
followed on after the arrival of David Sassoon in Baghdad from
Bombay, in the first half of the nineteenth century. David
Sassoon and the Sassoon family established many charities for
the Sephardis of Bombay, with the result that to-day they are a
comparatively rich community for that city.

These children—there were about twenty of them, the girls,
exceptionally for Oriental groups, being in the majority—were
extremely outspoken, and most entertaining. At first a little
shy, they started talking all at once when I asked them how
they lived at home, how they came to Israel, and other questions.

They told me that in Bombay they had been well off—better

off than in Israel. They all attended the same school there and had decided to come to Israel on account of a talk which was given to their school by a Zionist speaker. They had made up their minds to leave India as soon as they heard this speech. At first their parents protested strongly, but later on they agreed to let them go. The school was completely emptied by their departure and had to be shut down.

They related all this with a great deal of humour, with hand-clappings and many interruptions of each other. "What was it in the speech that made you think you ought to come?" I asked. "We went because of our religion," said one of the girls. "And what happened when you got to Israel?" "We lost our religion," grinned a boy who was something of the leading wit throughout our conversation. They all laughed.

"How do you like being in a Kibbutz in a Youth Aliyah Group?"

"We like it, but we are not satisfied," said a boy.

"Why not?"

"We do not consider that it gives us sufficient scope for our individual development."

One of the girls protested hotly at this. I asked the boy to explain what he meant.

"Here we are being trained to be farm labourers. That is all anyone is interested in. But we want to be different things."

"What, for example?"

"Well, I would like to be an engineer," said one of the boys.

"And I a scientist," said another.

"I would like to be a philosopher," said a third.

The others laughed at the third one, and said: "Do not take any notice of him." He had a very pale skin, wore spectacles, and looked rather ill.

I discussed the problems of the philosopher a little with him—they were concerned with his difficulties in obtaining books—and then I asked the group what they intended to do when they left the Kibbutz.

"Start a new Kibbutz of our own," said the girls excitedly. "Where?"

"We don't know until the government has given us the land for it."

"Perhaps in the Negev."

The boys disagreed. They did not seem nearly so fixed on the idea of starting a Kibbutz. They said they had quite other ideas. One or two of them wanted to go to the town.

Then they started saying that despite their attitude, they had learned a great deal from Youth Aliyah. They had been very stupid at first, they admitted, thinking that they were insulted by being asked to work on the land. But later they had realized that for an Israeli there was nothing humiliating about agriculture. They also felt that they had become a group—whereas when they arrived they were always quarrelling with one another. The boys thought that after they had been for a time in the army, they might after all want to start a Kibbutz and form the group once more.

"Another thing," one of the boys called out in his gay, amused voice, "there is racial prejudice in Israel—far more than there ever was in India. This one——" and he pointed to a boy who was particularly dark—"is always being called a nigger, when he goes away from the Kibbutz into the streets."

"And they have no idea here of how we live in India," another said. "They are completely ignorant. They are always asking us such stupid questions that we tell them anything that comes into our heads and they believe it."

"For instance, we tell them that in India we sleep in the tops of trees and only come down on to the ground during daylight."

"We tell them that when we walk in the streets of Bombay, each of us is accompanied by a lion and a tiger."

"And they believe every single thing we tell them," they boasted contemptuously.

One of the boys—Abraham, he was called—who had a particularly dark skin did not like to go outside the Kibbutz, because he was laughed at so much for being black, they said. The boy, who was extremely handsome, smiled sheepishly.

This group of children were delightful in their outspokenness and humour. An explanation for their remarkable frankness with me was that they were happy to speak the English language. In fact, one of the things they made a great point of was their objections to having to speak Hebrew.

Meeting them made me see the problem of the orientals in rather a new light. For, after all, these children had come, before their grandparents went to India, from exactly the same places as the Iraqi children now pouring into Israel. Yet they were completely Indianized, with a strong Anglo-Indian bias, because, being Jews, they had, until India's independence thought of themselves as close to the British.

They had been in India a hundred years, it is true, but this showed that in a century they could acquire the characteristics of another country. The problem of the orientals is soluble— given time. The question really is whether Israel has enough time and patience to await a long and sure development.

A few days later I was talking with some educators in a Kibbutz in the extreme north of the country. These educators were from England, and they had Moroccan children in their care. They expressed themselves about their charges so strongly that at the end of their remarks I said to them: "You have told me that the Moroccan children when they came here to you, had the following qualities: they lied, they stole, they attacked members of the Kibbutz with knives, they were distrustful, illiterate, uncultivated in every way, unco-operative and exhibitionistic. Do you mean to say they had no good qualities at all?"

"No. When they arrived here they had no good qualities. Now, thanks to our teaching them, they have a good many," was the very frank reply.

"They no longer steal so often, they lie less, they don't

attack you with their knives, they show more confidence, have learned Hebrew and writing and reading, are quieter and not quite such exhibitionists," said another.

"Could they draw?"

"Nothing to speak of. But we have taught them."

"Could they sing?"

"Only those miserable cacophonous noises."

Of course, I was a little shocked by the frankness of these educators. It would have soothed my psychoanalytical consciousness to be told that they had hidden virtues which had now been brought out, and that their wickedness had all been the result of suppressing these good qualities.

Yet on inquiry I discovered that eight of this particular group of children had been sentenced for criminal offences by the French police, and had come to Israel not so much in the role of immigrants as of *expulsées* from Morocco. Moreover, they did really now show a remarkable improvement.

A question which had long been in my mind was to ask what punishments were used with these children. As my interlocutors were so frank, I asked them this frankly. I followed up their answers with further inquiries, and formed a picture of what happened.

In most places, when the children arrived, the educators had tried to be enlightened and not punish them. But when the children hit and bit and threw stones at their hosts, or tried to knife them, they discovered that simply not to retaliate was not enough. They had to take a strong line or simply refuse to take any more of these children in the Kibbutzim. So they tried fighting back. From the moment that they did this, they found that the children had begun to respect and trust them. Soon it was possible to disarm in the matter of punishment on both sides.

Near Haifa, I visited the Yemenite Youth Aliyah Group in Nahlath-Yehudah.

Supervisor of these children was a famous educator known to friends of Youth Aliyah simply as "Ruth," the recipient of some very charming letters, which have been published, from Yemenite children.

The metaphors which these children employ show immediately — even in the English translation—that these people think in a language of concrete images derived from the Bible. Their thoughts express themselves spontaneously in parables.

A girl called Levana writes to Ruth:

"I want to tell you about what I was like in Yemen.

"I was a child who didn't know the difference between good and bad. I was like a tree in the desert that has no taste and no smell. Our rabbi in the Yemen was like a blind man who sends his son to the market. The son doesn't know the way, and the blind father leads him until they both lose their way."

Or take this letter—not written to Ruth, but to Henrietta Szold. It was found among Miss Szold's papers after her death. It is a boy's account of the circumstances which led him to leave the Yemen:

"And we lived in peace for several years until there came a new king. He was a wicked king who oppressed his subjects. The Arabs became infuriated and wanted to take revenge, but as they did not have to turn against the king's men, they decided to kill my father. They poisoned him, and after three days of pain he died. The Arabs wanted to divide my father's property among themselves. But the king heard of it, and he came with his soldiers and with his camels and his asses, and he took title to the land that had belonged to my father. He forced his way into our house and took all our belongings and showed no mercy to us. He beat my mother and he sent us to prison without thought that we were children."

And, in a letter which shows the impact of more sophisticated tastes, a boy called Abraham writes to Ruth:

"Also we must have a radio because we don't know what is

happening in the world. We want to hear it speak, and hear how it shouts, and know how to open it. You know if we are not happy, we cannot learn. But we have nothing to be happy with and in the evening everyone goes to his own room and is angry that he has nothing to be happy with."

After this, one is a little sad that they want a radio. However, one can trust Ruth. She is one of those rare people who has a real respect for the intrinsic qualities of the children. She wants to learn from them as much as to teach them.

In one of the rooms of this Yemenite children's village there is a collection of drawings and modelling done by these children. The models, made in clay, are of the cooking utensils, pots and jars which the Yemenites use in their own country. They look like the primitive pottery of a very old civilization; which is, of course, what they really are. The models are made with great skill and a strong sense of beauty.

The drawings illustrated the journey of the children from the Yemen into Israel. A line cork-screwing snake-like from side to side of the paper and back again, indicated (to the despair of many of the educators) the course of the journey. At the bottom of the page, the place of their departure was shown by a drawing of their village in the Yemen: mud houses and huts in the desert. Next were the children departing to the aeroplane. Then the aeroplane spiralling across mountains and desert, till at the top of the page it reached the airport, where it was met by a car and lots of soldiers. Lastly there was the arrival at a large town with many buildings.

All this was drawn very flat without perspective and with images which were symbols expressing the idea of the different points and incidents of the journey which had impressed themselves on the children. The style was reminiscent of Assyrian bas reliefs in the British Museum.

Some weeks after I had seen these drawings I attended an address given by a distinguished Israeli visitor to England, in which he referred to the problems of teaching the Yemenite children. He illustrated a difficulty by explaining that when they arrived it was difficult to make them understand the concept of a map. They had no idea in their minds of distances between places, direction, and position on a plan. They saw only a symbolic picture of places which had certain associations for them. A journey to them was a succession of emotional experiences, not of relations of points to one another in space. "The only way I could explain the idea of a map to a child was to point out to him that he and I sitting in our chairs were at a certain distance from one another and at a certain angle in relation to each other and to the other objects in the room, which one could indicate by points on a piece of paper, without having to draw an ideograph depicting the two of us on our chairs," he said.

This was all very true, and yet when he talked about the immense difficulty of getting these children out of their habit of visualizing situations too concretely, I could not help wondering whether he was not a little too assured in his assumption of the superiority of the power of making abstractions, over that of creating symbols. Of course, the fact is that a map is useful to us, in a way in which a drawing cannot be. It is necessary in a modern society to know about maps. So, of course, he was right in saying there was a difficulty. He might have been a little more humble about it, that is all.

The Yemen of the Jews was a culture which was as completely wiped out when the Yemenites got into the aeroplanes which took them to Israel as were the Arab villages of which all but the walls are destroyed. These aeroplanes did not surprise the Yemenites greatly—for had not the Bible prophesied that they would be borne back to the Promised Land on the silver wings of eagles? The bus at the air terminal when they arrived was their first disillusionment. It did not take to its wings and fly.

They themselves also provided the Israelis with some shocks, worse even than their inability to conceptualize maps. As when the pilot of one of the "silver eagles" looked round and saw his passengers calmly lighting a fire on the floor of the cabin, while preparing a ritualistic meal.

Ruth told me that the Yemenite children once they have begun to learn, despite their past ignorance, develop a passion for knowledge, particularly the science which explains the cause of thunder, and that the earth is round. If one of them by chance misses a lesson, he is furious and tries to make the educator give it to him again, in private. Children have been known to form a queue outside the classroom four hours before a lesson, for fear of missing it.

The children, since I could not speak Hebrew, decided to act a little play before me, to illustrate their life. It is their habit to make up such plays for one another.

The theme of the play was that the children now despised the witch doctors whose precepts they had accepted in the Yemen, having been liberated from superstition by enlightened medicine.

Three actors took part in this play which was done in the classroom without scenery, except for the large rack from which they hung the intimidating hooks, spikes, nails, animals' teeth, pincers and so on, which were the witch doctor's stock in trade. The witch doctor wore a magnificent white robe, with head dress and skirt edged at the bottom with a wide border. A frightened looking boy came in who was the patient. He made obeisance to the witch doctor who roared at him; the patient then described his symptoms. The witch doctor made incantations and decided that the patient should be cured by applying a red-hot iron to his stomach to "drive out the devil." The patient was then carried out—dead. The play ended with a short epilogue in which the moral that the children had formerly believed in witch doctors who treated them in this way and that they now benefited from kindly science, was underlined.

The play, without losing its satiric farcical quality, was yet acted with great dignity and natural grace, and the declamations of the witch doctor sounded magnificent.

After this, the boy who had been the witch doctor did some "character" dancing in which he imitated a priest, a rich man, a grovelling beggar, an Arab, etc.

In Israel everyone likes the Yemenites. They are the exceptions among the Orientals often used to illustrate the rule that the others are not so nice. Certainly it is difficult not to like this vivid and simple people.

CHAPTER XIII

A
MIDDLE EAST PINNACLE OF SCIENCE

THE Weizmann Institute, with the Hebrew University, raises the intellectual standards of the whole Middle East. It is one of the greatest and best equipped centres of research in the world. That it should carry on its work in this particular part of the world, is of great importance.

The Institute is situated on the outskirts of the town of Rehovoth on a main road from Tel Aviv to Jerusalem. This is an area of fruit trees, woods and fields. There are wide views across a flat landscape glistering with leaves, and the sharply white walls of new settlements.

Twenty years ago, the grounds of the Institute, with its lawns and flower beds and its avenue passing through a tunnel of the boughs of trees with which it is lined, was a sandy desert waste.

In the brochure explaining the aims of the Institute, there is written:

"The first scientific Institute in a totally new country carries an immense responsibility of a moral, social and intellectual order. Quite apart from the contribution which it may make, or fail to make, to the solution of particular problems, it sets a stamp, one which it will be difficult to erase, on the entire moral and intellectual development of the country. If it is successful, it gives a permanent creative turn to the new country; if it is a failure, its continuation or abandonment is equally a discouragement affecting whole decades or generations."

The Institute fuses two ideas of Dr. Weizmann and his

colleagues of the Zionist movement. One was to create a centre of pure research in a country deeply involved in practical problems; the other was to apply this research where it branched out into discoveries which could be useful to the country. In the Weizmann Institute, Israel has been given a brain centre capable both of disinterested contemplation and also of applying this spirit of detachment to practical problems.

Weizmann and his colleagues were evidently preoccupied with the question of the kind of country that Israel would be in its Middle Eastern environment. When projecting a research centre twenty years ago, they probably thought of the future State as a country where Jewish intelligence would be used to perfect techniques of small-scale industrial production in an environment predominantly agricultural. Israel was to be a kind of Switzerland of this part of the world: rural but with a few specialized small industries, not requiring great industrial towns nor massive imports of raw materials.

It does not look as if the new State will turn out to be like this, yet the importance of the Weizmann Institute is none the less great; perhaps it is even more needed in a country which certainly falls into no neat pattern however much it is planned.

I spent two days at the Weizmann Institute and was shown round the laboratories by the research workers. They explained their work to me with gifts of lucid exposition I have not encountered previously among scientists. As I have never been able to understand the simplest scientific experiment, this was a revealing and rather disturbing experience.

Looking at an immensely complicated apparatus called the mass spectrometer, consisting of many glass tubes, retorts, jars and batteries strung together—with burners distributed under retorts at strategic points—I actually had the illusion, lasting for a few seconds, that I understood how an atom was weighed. Other hallucinations I underwent were: that I understood the principles on which heavy water is isolated; and the mechanism whereby water-soluble polymers coil or uncoil, contract or expand, according to whether alkali or acid are added to them in a solution. Since this mechanism may explain how the muscles of a living organism work, it is one of the pieces of research at the Institute which has excited the most interest.

However, I had better not try to recapture my moments of insight into things which I did not understand. Instead, I can perhaps explain in a general way the principles and the work of the Institute.

First, then, the principles.

The scientists are very conscious that their main work is to carry on pure research. It is necessary for them to be insistent about this. For if once they gave way to the pressure which is brought on them to make the Institute into a research station for seeking solutions of the day to day practical problems which arise in Israel, the scientists who have come from all over the world here would be diverted from their main lines of research, and would be concerning themselves with immediate problems of less scientific importance.

And this would mean that the best scientists would not stay at the Institute. For a scientist less than anyone can afford to be diverted from his vocation of inquiring into the particular problem which interests him and which he is qualified to undertake, in order to become a mere journalist of science. For him to do this would mean his sacrificing something which he alone can do, for something which a great many others can do; and beyond this it would mean sacrificing to a particular situation and occasion something which may be of interest to the development of science as a whole.

Secondly, the work.

When one comes to look at the actual work being done in the buildings of the Institute, one sees that in practice a kind of compromise between pure research and practical projects is arrived at. It is a compromise which does not compromise anyone, for the research workers go on with their research whereas the people occupied with the study of particular Israeli problems work independently.

Pure research is chiefly into proteins, water-soluble polymers, fermentation processes (carrying on the work for which Dr. Weizmann is famous as a scientist) and applied mathematics.

These fields of research do, for the most part, open on to potentialities of more practical work. For example, the research into proteins is connected with the discovery of new synthetic foods (obviously most important for Israel), and the study of water-soluble polymers is connected with the research of nylon-like substances; while efficient substitute fuels and artificial rubber better than real rubber may be developed as the result of research into fermentation processes.

I was less out of my depth in looking at the practical research which was going on. For example, in the first laboratory I entered, Dr. Esther Hellinger (of London University), surrounded by racks of test tubes (each of which contained a little section of straw in a solution), was studying the retting of flax. Her problem was to discover the conditions (of solution, temperature, etc.) in which the fibres break away from the stalk most quickly and produce the strongest and shiniest kind of flax.

In an adjoining laboratory, Dr. Anna Weizmann, sister of the President was analyzing the properties of Israeli plants. She showed me a flask of blue oil, transparent and the colour of ink, which she had extracted from a plant called *artemesia arborescence*. This liquid contained azulaine and camphor.

The main practical problem of Israel is that of obtaining water, especially in the Negev, the southern part of the country, where even such water as can be obtained by boring wells, often turns out to be brackish. At the Weizmann Institute, a large machine has been constructed which successfully filters brackish water, producing a very pure water. Unfortunately though, the filters of the machine accumulate large quantities of salt, and they can only be cleaned with sulphuric acid—an expensive process.

On the roof of a building adjoining that which contains the syphoning machine, there are several delightful gadgets. One is a model windmill consisting of horizontal flaps attached to two parallel vertical chains; the wind lifts up the flaps and the chains rotate, turning a cog as they do so, just as a chain turns the wheel of a bicycle. When the flaps lifted by the wind reach the top and move in the downwards direction, they fall, until they have rotated to the windward and upward moving side again.

On this roof there were also various experimental devices for purifying salt or brackish water; by making it, for example, condense on a sloping glass roof through which the sun shone upon a patch of water covered by the glass. The condensed water then flows down the side of the glass into a gutter through which it flows into a receptacle. But like all the other schemes I have seen for purifying water, this is too expensive to be practicable.

Chemists at the Institute are occupied in research into new narcotics—the practical importance of inventing new anaesthetics and pain-alleviating drugs, needs no dwelling on.

An example of pure research which has its very practical aspect is the experiments made at the Institute into cancer-producing subjects.

The opposite of this is something highly practical which, contrariwise, has little practical application—the study of living organisms found in the Dead Sea. The astonishing thing about these very elementary forms of life is that they exist at all. They show that life is possible under conditions where no one had expected it.

Part of the practical work of the Institute is making a survey of the geological potentialities of the country. Here they have carried out the preliminary research into areas where oil is likely to be found in Israel, in the Negev, and also near Haifa.

There are typical formations where oil may be found, but it will not be possible to find whether it is there until borings have been made; and this is an expensive process.

A survey has also been made of the Negev, where phosphates and glass sand exist in large quantities. There are also deposits of manganese, gypsum, mica and feldspar. Since I left Israel I have read of iron ore also being found.

The castor plant which grows very easily on the soil of Israel, may prove to be one of the country's chief assets. For castor oil has been found by the research workers at the Sieff Institute (which is attached to the Weizmann Institute) to be the basis of a nylon-like material, claimed to be in some ways superior to nylon. Castor oil plants can also be broken down into eneanthol and undecylenic acid, which could be important by-products of a castor plant industry.

The object of research here is how to grow castor plants which are of the same height, so that they can be mechanically harvested, since at present the harvesting is very costly.

In Rehevoth, as in other parts of Israel, the people dream dreams; and one of these is that the world is on the verge of a great shifting of its centres of raw materials. The fuels and artificial rubber obtained by the development of fermentation processes, may prove more useful than coal mines and rubber plants. Plastics may replace many metals and woods. Beyond this there lie hopes of making fertile the southern Negev desert which is half of Israel's territory, and perhaps even—as Lewis Mumford foretold 25 years ago in his book *Technics and Civilization*, of obtaining power directly from the great and constant heat of the sun in the Middle East. In this century we may indeed see a shifting of the sources of raw materials and energy.

CHAPTER XIV

THE NEGEV

THE last trip of my superficial journeys in Israel was to the Negev. I went accompanied by Mr. Michaelis, the husband of Eva Michaelis who had been so kind to me in Jerusalem on my several journeys.

We drove from Rehevot to Shefeya run by two Americans, Mr. and Mrs. Rappoport. At this Children's Village, they have specialized in teaching the children to play on stringed instruments, mostly guitars, and a few recorders. We listened to a charming concert, the highlight of which was a performance of Haydn's Toy Symphony.

In the morning we got up at 4 a.m. and drove to Beer-Sheba where we had arranged to join another party touring the Negev.

As it happened though, we did not join this party, but were taken by a young business man who had an interest in the potash and glass sand mines which are being developed in the desert. Probably this tour with a man who was vitally concerned with these developments was more revealing than an official tour might have been.

Beer-Sheba is a straggling pioneer town which puts me in mind not so much of the seven wells dug by Abraham (which were actually at Tel-Es-Sab, east of modern Beer-Sheba), as of a Wild West movie of some pioneering town in California during the previous century. It has the wide dust main road running through it, on either side of which are low-lying shack-like bars, cafés and shops, a few side streets where there are a hotel, and small flat-roofed, one-storeyed houses. The hotel at which we stayed consisted of a few rooms built round a patio, and two or three showers and W.C.s along the side of a corridor. There was no dining room, only a passageway entrance which served as the reception centre. We ate at what we considered to be the best of the cafés along the main road, where the other guests, in open-necked rough shirts, and torn, dusty trousers, and with guns at their hips, sprawled in the wooden chairs.

At moments it all suggested to me that the Jews—who love acting out their lives—themselves wished Beer-Sheba to resemble a Wild West movie. Still, it could hardly have looked anything else, since the prescription for pioneering at the edge of deserts is simply to combine the greatest air of adventure and excitement with the completest minimum of everything else. Moreover, Beer-Sheba was completely lacking in the violent, roaring, hard-drinking, whoring side of the Wild West. There was nothing except a little weak beer to drink, everyone was well-behaved, and all the guests in our hotel were tucked up in bed by 10 o'clock.

Beer-Sheba is the chief pioneering town of Israel. Here money is made quickest, and labour is most expensive. But Beer-Sheba is also a show place, the hub of the Negev, with the flowering desert of plains north-west of it and the unredeemed desert to the south. Tourists are brought here to see what Israelis have already done and to imagine what they intend to do. Loads and loads of young people from the Kibbutzim and from Youth Aliyah are brought here to train or to work in the desert.

Whatever its potentialities, the Negev is the most important symbol in Israel to-day for that very considerable section of the population which believes the wilderness really can be made fertile, that waters can break out of rocks, that minerals of great worth lie about in forgotten and neglected places and that an Old Testament miracle can be reborn within a modern scientific one. The Negev is the historic challenge to Israel stated geographically, if not exactly personified. It is the half of the country which is quite unused and which therefore offers this little nation the chance to double its territory.

Our guide, the young engineering business man, said he did not think that Israel could exist without the Negev: and he, I was to discover, was almost cynical about much of what he saw there. The Negev combines all the dreams and all the demands on will and action and scientific purpose of the country within one situation which everyone can see. It exists to prove or disprove the faith which Melitz had put to me within a few hours of my arrival at Haifa: "I am sure they will strike oil in the Negev." Perhaps not oil, but perhaps many other things.

That morning we were only one of many carloads of tourists going to see the Negev. When we had returned, hot and dusty in the evening, after our supper I walked through the streets of Beer-Sheba and saw lorry-load on lorry-load of young people arriving from the Kibbutzim, in order to go far out into the desert for their training.

Until 1948, Beer-Sheba was Arab, but during the war the Arabs abandoned it. Its present population is about 22,000 and there is every sign of its growing rapidly.

Access to the area south of Beer-Sheba is only allowed if you have a government permit from the "Negev Commission." You are required also to provide yourself with oil, water, food and weapons.

In the Negev itself there is a nomadic population of about 48,000, mostly Bedouins. Arabs often infiltrate into the desert and attack the Jews. Only two days before my tour, some Jewish youths had been killed in an ambush.

After an altogether exceptional breakfast (we each had two fried eggs and the coffee was passable) in the main road café, we went in a south-westerly direction, past the police post (they examined our permit) and along a fairly good road through country in which pasture-land gradually merged into and became indistinguishable from scrub, and then the scrub gradually gave way to rock and sand, until we came to a place consisting only of two houses, for desert police, called Kurnub.

Beyond Kurnub the desert became both more sandy and more hilly, and the scrub very sparse among the rocks. Occasionally in the distance we saw bedouins with their camels like moving humps of the brown-coloured desert itself, moving through the landscape.

The road needs describing, for it is an important factor in the development of the Negev, since without a good road the minerals which are found cannot be transported.

In every sense of the word, the road was uneven. A few miles of it would be completed, and we would bowl along them over a smooth tarmac surface. Then we would come to a stretch of nothing except a foundation of broken stones; here the road, being unfinished was, of course, quite impassable, so we had to drive alongside it on a desert track. Then the road would stop altogether for a few miles and there would be nothing except the track.

A great many vehicles had gone along this track already, with the result that ruts were worn so deeply into the sand that sometimes our car was straddled on the hump between the ruts, with wheels unable to touch the ground on either side. This, though, was not so bad as the places where the track went across rocks, in which there were also very deep ruts. For here the chassis would crash down on to some protruding rock in the centre of the track, with the whole weight of the car. Our petrol tank was dented and shifted several inches, but we were lucky enough not to break an axle.

The young engineer business man who had invited us with him was from Poland, though he had spent a good deal of his life in England, having been educated there. He had a pale complexion and dark hair, and the almost classical features of certain handsome Poles. Apart from a certain air of nobility and veiled suffering, he did not look Jewish at all.

He was a patriotic Israeli in a very fed-up state of mind. He became eloquent about the road: understandably, since he had the prospect before him of transporting potash over it. He was angry in the first place because he had been told it was nearly finished. He kept on congratulating himself bitterly that he had come along to see how things really were, as you never have the slightest idea, he said, from what they tell you, and even from what they mark on their charts.

He was even more upset by the patches of good road than by the great stretches of bad or unbuilt. As he pointed out, the road which was being built consisted of a single layer of broken stones laid directly on to the desert with, over that, a layer of gravel and tarmac. The stones were not of the best quality, and one layer of them was not enough, in any case. Within a few weeks, heavy traffic would dent through the surface of the road and make ruts which would soon be as deep as those along the tracks where we had driven. If this were so, he asked, how could an industry in which lorries had to transport several scores of tons of glass sand and potash every day over this road, be established?

He explained that the importance of this road had greatly increased since 1948. For, before the establishment of the Jewish State, the potash from Sodom at the southern end of the Dead Sea was transported by motor-boat to the northern end, and thence by road the short way to Jerusalem. But the northern end is now in Jordan.

One could certainly understand this young man's feeling of exasperation, bordering on despair.

We were stopped by three road builders who asked us to take them to their encampment further along the road. They were a French-speaking Jew from Alexandria, recently immigrated, a Druse from Galilee, and an Arab from Abu Gosh, a village in Israel, near Jerusalem.

Our friend complained to them about the roads, and then they in turn complained about their work. What was the use of working, the one from Egypt said, if, having earned I£125 a

month, he then had to pay I£20 of it back to the government in
income tax? He said, too, that his wages were worth far less
than would seem according to the official calculations of the
cost of living on which they were based.

He did not seem to take Mr. Michaelis's suggestion that it
was not necessary to use the black market as intended seriously.

Wages in the Negev for unskilled or semi-skilled labour vary
between I£3 10s. and I£5 a day. Meals and their shelter at night
in their encampment are also provided for the workers.

Of course, the Israeli I£ is worth much less than our £, and its
value is decreasing all the time (for example the cost of living
went up 6 or 7 per cent. in the three months following the day
when I had this conversation). Nevertheless, the roadmender's
wages compared favourably with the I£140 a month (without
expenses) of a professor at the Hebrew University. In Israel
an efficient carpenter can easily earn I£10 a day.

The roadmakers were friendly and invited us to eat with them
at their encampment at a bend in the road where the road was
cut between two hills.

We ate at a hut constructed very roughly of wooden boards.
It was extremely hot and full of flies which swarmed over
everything. Our hosts were Iraqis, Egyptians and people of
one or two other nationalities. They explained to us with pride
that they had a French chef; and certainly the cook, who spoke
French, provided a meal which was surprisingly good. It
consisted of a boiling hot vegetable soup, followed by beans,
olives and potatoes. It was remarkably clean, considering all
the flies. "The best African cooking," a Moroccan immigrant
proudly commented.

After this meal, we continued along a road as far as a settlement called Camp C, the last habitation of the road-builders.
From here the distance to Sodom is about 16 kilometres. It is
300 metres above sea level and across the falling broken ground,
you see the southern end of the Dead Sea, 400 metres below
sea level. In the harsh white glare of mid-day, everything looked

bare and grey, and beyond the rocks and stones of the hill-side near us, the Dead Sea was a wedge of pure shadow in the low-lying, uneven, vegetation-less surroundings which looked like enormous fragments of fibrous shale lying on their sides and overlapping one another. Beyond them on the further side of the lake were once more the flowing turquoise lines of the hills of Jordan.

At Camp C we ran into a party of high government officials on a tour of inspection—the Accountant-General, the Director of Inland Revenue, the Director-General of the Ministry of Labour, and others. This gave our friendly guide an opportunity, which he did not hesitate to seize, to take one of them aside and give his views about roads. The road—now I come to think of it—in addition to everything else, was not wide enough. Just another six inches, he had said, would have made all the difference.

We drove back to Kurnub, and then turned south to an area called—appropriately enough—the Great Depression: Mahtesh Hagadol. The road approaching this canyon winds through high hills of sand and sandstone, absolutely without foliage. The lack of any familiar natural object whereby to measure them has the effect of making them look enormous, and one has the impression of being at the bottom of the burning pit. If art imitates life, these hills owe much to the influence of the cubists and abstractionists. One hill with a large sandstone boulder just below its crest was doing a very good imitation of some piece of sculpture called "Cone giving birth to a sphere."

When you get to the canyon itself, the effects are more surrealist than abstract or cubist. The depression itself resembles an immense irregularly shaped floor—like a parade ground—surrounded by bastion-shaped walls which are the height of the surrounding landscape below which the canyon has sunk. From the walls there are protrusions carved to fantastic shapes, the sawn-off edge of a picture frame, or the lower half of a violin.

This is a landscape of Milton's *Paradise Lost*, full of brimstone and sulphur, rather than a dwelling with well-ordered heating arrangements, like Dante's Inferno. You would expect it to be inhabited by pterodactyls and prehistoric reptiles. It is very difficult to imagine it being redeemed.

It is the wilderness which caused the Children of Israel to murmur and become rebellious against Moses. It is certainly a difficult place to feel any affection for. My companions, filled with their picture of the flowering Negev desert, and perhaps remembering the bad record of this place in their nation's history, fell silent. Mr. Michaelis went back to Beer-Sheba in a serious and thoughtful mood. It was not I think that such a formidable picture of the worst possible desert had discouraged him: for no one, I suppose, imagines that this part of the Negev can become fertile. His reason for being depressed was perhaps just the sense of being in the presence of something ominous; ultimately, it was the same reaction as the more sensitive European Jews betray in their voices when they talk of the khamsin or the locusts.

We returned to Beer-Sheba, where we took showers, rested a little and then went out to sup at the "best" café, where we had eaten eggs that morning. At a nearby table was a group of strikingly handsome young people, some of them dressed in Biblical robes. They were looking at photographs, and soon we realized that these were stills of a movie about the forty years in the wilderness. The director of the movie showed me photographs of Rachel, Moses, Aaron and other Biblical characters, in some of the scenery through which we had been moving. They were so much more appropriate to this desert than ourselves and the people around us in our torn shirts and dusty trousers, that—being dazed by the sun—I got this project mixed up in my mind for a moment with those for reforming the Negev, and wondered whether these were pictures for a projected sojourn in the wilderness or of one that had taken place many years ago.

N

In the course of the day, we had seen one or two of the projects. There was a pit containing glass sand, and nearby an open place containing clay of the kind from which the cruder forms of ceramics—wash-basins and the like—can be made.

As our guide pointed out to us, however, the cost of taking this glass sand to Haifa is considerably more at the present moment than of bringing glass sand all the way from Belgium by ship. To lower the cost depends on improving the roads.

A new ceramics factory is being built near Beer Sheba, and the caolinite clay which we had seen will be used there, and can be transported there cheaply even under present conditions.

On the following day, we went to see the north-western Negev, which was much more encouraging.

Still accompanied by our business friend, we drove north-west on the main Beer Sheba-Gaza road for about twenty kilometres, and then turned west to B'eri a large kibbutz, founded in 1940 at a time when it was in the midst of Arab territory.

This western plain of the Negev is extremely flat. It is like a Dutch landscape transported to the eastern Mediterranean, and has the curious luminous quality which the Dutch painters noted in their country. Under an immense sky the flat land, like a mirror made up of different surfaces and different colours, reflects the light in a hundred different subtle ways. Any straight lines which are seen at once suggest huge perspectives. On the morning when we went there, the light was rather diffused and silvery-whitish, perhaps as the result of the amount of dust suspended in the air. Parts of the landscape where there was ripening or ripened corn, shone like wide expanses of pale gold leaf in the light which blurred out almost every detail except variations of luminosity. Barley fields shone whitish like the colour of the turning leaves of poplars. Occasional clusters of palm-trees, cactus-hedges, farmsteads and flattened walls of broken Arab villages were like breakwaters emerging above this plain, becalmed like a flat sea, wrinkled only by a few scratches left by the tracks of vehicles.

During the war, all the Arabs left this part of the Negev, and, after the founding of the new State, water was brought here by pipes from the Galilean hills.

We travelled for many miles through fields where there were grain, potatoes and onions. On our way to Beeri we picked up an American immigrant, who told us that he was one of eighty who had formed a new kibbutz, called Urim, in this area. Urim, he said, had now been connected to the water pipe-line and for the past few months the kibbutz had been able to engage in irrigated agriculture.

At Beeri we looked for the sulphur mines, which are marked on the map, without success, almost getting ourselves arrested by running over the Egyptian frontier.

So we drove back to Beeri and then went northwards to Migdal Gad, a town populated by 13,000 new immigrants. It is near to what remains of the famous crusading town of Ascalon, whose ruins are on the coast, buried for the most part under sand dunes. We looked at the sand dunes and then went to a mosque, in whose cool, refreshing courtyard were relics of Roman, Arab and Crusaders' architecture.

CHAPTER XV

A SUM BUT NOT A SUMMING UP

I HAVE tried to take the reader with me on some brief visits to places; I have invited him to read over my shoulder some information about Youth Aliyah; and I have thrown ideas at him which crossed my mind during this journey.

Having ideas about places and people one doesn't know very well, is perhaps inexcusable. Yet not quite so; because there is always the possibility that a first reaction may be one of which familiarity would have made one unaware; and wrong ideas which are freshly stated, may jog the reader to find the right ones for himself.

Anyway, there is a certain need to form impressions into a whole picture. So in this last chapter I am under an obligation to put my impressions in a certain order.

The children were a good introduction to Israel, because their lives are the material out of which the State will create either its unity or its disunity. That the Israelis take the children seriously, does more perhaps to show they are serious than do their politics, which they take so solemnly.

All the same, if the future depends on the children, the children also depend upon the present situation. If the new country is overrun, or if it sinks into economic chaos, then the lives of these children will show the misery of the present decade.

So study of the children inevitably leads to consideration of other things. Here, in my last chapter, I want to sum up my wider impressions of Israel; not a summing up, which I am not qualified to make, but the setting down of a sum whose result I do not know. This will also lead me to touch on something which I have only referred to until now, except in the case of the potential "colour division" in Israel; the deep divisions which are at the back of Israeli politics.

The most obvious thing that strikes every visitor to Israel, is the disastrous economic situation. The significance of this will be clear at once to the English reader—long familiar with the struggle to balance imports with exports—when he is told that Israel's imports exceed her exports at least five times.

At the beginning of 1952, Ben Gurion, the Prime Minister, in the speech in which he introduced the New Economic Policy, said that "Ingathering, Security and Development had required, in the period from the beginning of 1949 to December, 1951, imports of no less than I£296 millions (about 828 million dollars), whereas exports amounted to only I£37.4 million. The difference had to be covered by various drives, loans, grants and other forms of capital transfer."*

He went on to point out that a large proportion of imports had been machinery for capital goods; and to add that nonetheless a great deal had also been for consumer goods. Then he drew the moral—which will surprise no English reader—that Israelis must pay in exports for what they import.

The situation of Israel's balance of payments is an extreme example of the malady which also affects Britain. That it is extreme Israelis recognize in one of their wise-cracks: "If only we were as badly off as the English, then things would be much better."

However, one circumstance makes the situation of Israel rather different. Israel's predicament is the vital concern of world Jewry, for which saving Israel is a real crusade. From this point of view Israel is like an investment made by a larger concern than itself: an extremely expensive and unprofitable investment, but one which cannot, in honour bound, be

*Zion, Volume II, No. 10, 11, Jan-Feb., 1952.

liquidated, and to which the larger interest is attached by inescapable moral obligations.

So Israel has more backing than would appear if one judged her situation simply by the export-import situation. With her, the imponderables which are and will continue to be of decisive importance as material advantages, are very great indeed.

All the same, the very bad present situation exists at a time when World Jewry is already making immense efforts; in fact, without those efforts, it is difficult to see how the new State could continue another day. This shows also that even with those efforts the situation remains very bad.

World Jewry may make even greater efforts, and probably will do so. Despite the tensions between the Jews inside and those outside Israel (which may lead to a temporary worsening of the situation if either side succeeds in annoying the other too much), the Jewish State would make no sense unless, in a supreme crisis, it could count on World Jewry to make a supreme effort, even exceeding what has been done up to now. The reasons for irritation are finally dissolved in the justice which is, from the Zionist point of view, the foundation of the Jewish State. In the final analysis, the behaviour of the Israelis to-day does not affect this situation; Israel is more important as a fact than is the behaviour of the present generation of Israelis.

With all this, though, the economy of Israel is so basically unsound that it is difficult to think of it becoming balanced even within 20 or 30 years. Unfortunately it seems that Israel has not so much time as this at its disposal. The new State cannot afford to remain for a generation in the wilderness. The 40 years has to be cut down—everyone apparently agrees— to five.

There is just a possibility that all the forces within and outside Israel will not be able to save the State from disaster. People friendly to Israel who have reviewed all the facts are driven back in the end to expressions of faith in the mission of Israel which they cannot but believe will overcome all difficulties.

Here again the English should have a profound understanding of Israel's situation. For we, who have also lived through years when it could be demonstrated by every disinterested intelligent observer that we had almost no chance of survival, will understand the solid sense of falling back on a foundation of obstinate faith, when all the facts seem against survival.

Added to all the economic problems there is one vast problem, itself partly economic, but also political and cultural, which adds immeasurably to the difficulties of Israel. That is the Ingathering itself.

As Ben Gurion pointed out in the same speech to the Knesset, the Israeli parliament, the Jewish population of Israel had increased "from 650,000 in 1948 to nearly one and a half million, 684,275 of whom were new immigrants."*

The majority of these immigrants were, as I have pointed out, from Asia and Africa, the so-called "Oriental" Jews. That they should have been the majority is inevitable, for the creation of the new State which led to its immediate invasion by the surrounding Arab countries, also led to waves of persecution against the Jewish population in the Arab countries.

The fact that more than half the population consists of these new immigrants means inevitably that a majority of the Jews in Israel are now almost unacquainted with the aims of the Zionist founders of the State.

The pioneers, who correspond to the Pilgrim Fathers and the New England Puritans in American history, are now in a distinct minority. The continuity of their work and their ideas will be found (when we are able to look back on this period), to have been not so much broken as flooded over by the inpouring of the new life of people with different aspirations,

---

* Ibid.

fewer ideals and perhaps worse ideas, but who have the immense force of their own wishes.

American history provides several examples of how the
flooding in of new immigrants has altered the balance of forces in
the country, thus breaking down the continuity of the culture
and of traditions which seemed rooted and established. It has
happened that within a few years leaders of thought have
suddenly found themselves isolated, frozen away in an exalted
climate where they have no contact with the crowds pouring
off the incoming ships. Those who should be the fathers,
suddenly find themselves, in their own lifetimes, the ancestors.

In Israel, this flooding in of new immigrants has happened
on a far greater scale within a far shorter time, before the ideals
of the pioneers had time to establish themselves and take root
in the life of the new State. Most of the recent immigrants
came into Israel with a primitive idea in their minds that it
would be the Promised Land of Milk and Honey where they
need do no work. They regarded manual labour as degrading
and perhaps the worst of their disillusionments in Israel was the
discovery that they were supposed to share the belief that the
new State should be a vast agricultural settlement.

Inevitably, they were, and will continue to be for many years,
a burden on a State already committed to such uneconomic
propositions as having to support a large army held in readiness
to defend itself against the threatened second wave of invasion
from the Arab countries.

Perhaps there is one good aspect of the new immigrants being
the "orientals." This is that the European Jews are aware of a
challenge to their ideas and therefore have to reconsider them
at a time when they certainly should be thought out again and
re-stated—at the beginning of the new State. They see very
clearly the dangers of their country becoming Levantine.
Although there is a risk of Israel being divided into two camps
of the Eastern and the Western elements, the chief hope of
avoiding ultimate confusion is in the European Jews taking the

lead, while at the same time trying to make themselves into one nation on equal terms with the Orientals.

One preliminary step to achieving the health for the State is peace and co-operation with the Arabs. It is difficult to think how Israel can really go forward without this. Yet it is perhaps of all existing problems the one least likely to be solved. In a country where people are optimistic about so many things, and even among people who agreed as to the urgency of settling the Jewish-Arab problem, no one I met offered the slightest hope that a settlement could be reached.

Having outlined the situation, and having agreed that it is necessary and reasonable to have faith, I believe that there can be no effective faith if the nation is divided against itself on fundamental issues. There must be a basic unity. So the next questions to attempt to answer are: What are the elements of disunity? and in what direction must one look for the unity on which faith can rest firmly?

Until now I have avoided politics, but now I shall have to refer to them, because it is in the political alignments that we can see most clearly the unifying or disuniting tendencies in a country.

Israeli politics express profound differences of political philosophy, of religion, and of conception of a way of life.

The political parties reflect the following divisions:—

(1) Religious divisions between orthodox and unorthodox.

(2) Ideological divisions between right and left of a kind with which Europeans are familiar.

(3) The ideological split between the theoreticians of the extreme left (Mapam) and the governmental Labour Party (Mapai).

(4) The Trades Union Movement (Histadrut) representing a vast monopoly of labour unions which forms a kind of State within the State.

These divisions go deeper than those between political parties in most democratic countries. One can only understand their depth if one takes into consideration such factors as the way of life to which the Orthodox Jews (for example) have clung for centuries: which would lead us to understand also its opposite, the liberation from an imprisoning orthodoxy felt by the agnostic Jews who have distinguished themselves in the sciences and arts as a result of precisely this liberation, even while (if they came to Israel) they have remained Zionists.

The divisions I have described are indoctrinated into the followers of the various parties during childhood. Education is conducted along Party lines. There are four educational systems in Israel. One is conducted by Labour (Mapai and Mapam); one by the General Zionists (right and centre parties); one by the Mizrachi Party (orthodox) ; and lastly one by Agudat Israel (ultra-orthodox).

In an article from which I have quoted these facts, Dov Jehoshua* points out that "Even the sports' movements correspond to parties, e.g., Maccabi (right of centre), Hapoel (left) and Betav (Herut, or extreme right nationalist)."

The Histadrut (Trades Union Federation) is perhaps the most powerful Trades Union Organization in the world. It was founded by the Workers' Movement of the Mapai, but as it has been developing within the day-to-day life of the Jewish settlements for nearly 30 years, before there was any question of the Mapai Party forming a government, it is far more embedded in the life of the country than is the government party. To quote Dov Jehoshua's article again: "The Histadrut is the most powerful factor in the country because it is not only a Trades Union Federation but—rather anomalously—is a capitalist organization engaging through various subsidiary companies in many types of industrial and commercial activity in the country. It has been accused of being a monopoly and,

---

* Ibid.

although not consciously striving towards this end, does in fact control many aspects of life in Israel."

The Ben Gurion Government represents a compromise between the orthodox religious conscience and the kind of day-to-day commonsensical socialism (which also compromises with free enterprise) which seems the almost inevitable form of government in the circumstances of Israel, if a clash between different sections of opinion is to be avoided.

So there is a government meeting day-to-day developments according to socialist principles tempered by respect for the sensibilities of the religious dogmatists, and for the individualism of the capitalists who fight against restrictions. Behind the government is the Histadrut, representing the interests of workers who want higher wages, better conditions and less work. They have pushed the working class cause to the point where workers form capitalist organizations of their own.

Beyond this there are the more or less extremist fanatics: the ultra-orthodox who would deprive everyone of meat sooner than import any that is not kosher, who are prepared to come out into the streets and cast stones at those who break the Sabbath, and who hedge their own lives and would hedge the lives of others round with the innumerable gins and snares of the Mosaic law. Then there are the unrealistic theorists of the Mapam—Zionists who would like to travel to Moscow—who attend May Day celebrations in their tractors given to them by American aid, draped round with red ribbons and with Communist slogans. There is Herut on the extreme right, whose nationalist violence makes some people shudder with memories of Hitlerism.

There are, of course, also moderates and liberals. But there are the divisions I have mentioned, and when one adds to them the potential race or colour division between Westerners and Orientals, the question arises: Where is unity to be found in Israel ?

Two things might provide the conditions making towards such unity.

The first is the general crisis through which the newly born State is passing.

The second is the potentiality always contained within the fact that the Jews in Israel are united within their being Jews.

Nations confronted with a crisis as great as that which Israel meets to-day, may react in one of two ways: either they fall apart, or there is a tendency for the most rigid divisions to be melted down, and for the nation to find unity within its searing experiences.

Although the divisions in Israel are so marked, none the less there are no signs of the nation falling apart. The government itself—unsatisfactory as such a coalition may be—represents a meeting of forces to deal with the crisis.

Doubtless there is a widespread feeling of discouragement in the young State four years after its birth. Such a reaction would be inevitable even had things turned out far better.

Some immigrants probably regret that they ever came to Israel. There are even a few who go away again; yet it is remarkable how few.

The split in the Left is a division which follows almost inevitably on the entry of a Labour movement into a coalition; and the crisis in the Kibbutzim is partly a reflection of the general economic crisis, partly the result of the increased importance of the towns in relation to the country.

It would seem that while there has been no breaking up, every group remains fixed in its own position (except for the government coalition). But in fact within these positions, concessions are made, and the extremists both of the orthodox right and the communist left, show signs of weakening influence. The extreme nationalists no longer command much hearing, and the Mapam is in danger of a split in its own ranks.

An important group which really does have claims to be non-party is the army. Every young person of either sex has to have military training, and the government and the army leaders have seized the opportunity to provide non-political non-sectarian education within the army. In the army to have extreme religious or political views is a tolerated eccentricity, not allowed to influence the exigencies of military life. Thus among recruits an attitude of unity is growing up which exists in no other training. As an instrument of education the army may have enormous importance. Moreover, the Israelis are enthusiastic soldiers.

The beating down of differences by the brute force of events is not enough in itself to provide national unity, though it might create the conditions for it.

Unity must lie in some conception of what it means to be a returned, ingathered Jew. This conception must be positive and not just the idea of "the exile from the exile." It should permit of variety of attitudes and of disagreement, so long as the singleness of the meeting place in which every Israeli is one with every other Israeli exists and is recognized.

For Jews scattered in the Diaspora, unity was the dispersal itself, with its concomitant vow of "we shall meet next year in Jerusalem." The Jew in Jerusalem who read about the persecution of the Jew in Warsaw felt at one with him.

But when the Jews were ingathered the universal quality which had bound them together, evaporated with the concretization of a dream. They were not victims and they were not persecuted any more. They were face to face with one another. And they found that most of the other faces looked different from what they had expected.

Of course, the orthodox Jew could say: "All would be made one if all were like me." But the fact is that all were not like him. Some were agnostic with the same intensity as he was religious.

Also (apart from peoples lost to modern civilization, like the Yemenites), the religion of some Jews, just as much as the un-religion of others, was the result of the exile. Many were religious because, without a very strict code, they would have been absorbed into the gentiles. They would have lost their identity, sacrificed the chances of their children and their children's children being ingathered, and borne in their actions the responsibility of the suicide of their race.

Others had become agnostic because they regarded such an attitude as a kind of voluntary ghetto. The irreligious could at least say they had achieved spiritual liberation for the Jewish consciousness which went forth to wonderful creative achievements recognized by gentiles and Jews alike. It was the agnosticism of the artistic Jews and their wonderful contributions to the arts and to humanist learning which made anti-semitism not merely inhuman and unchristian, but also a sign of cultural barbarism.

With the Ingathering some of the reasons for both religious orthodoxy and for austere agnosticism, have disappeared. The conditions which supported these no longer exist. The religious impulse to create an orthodoxy which preserved the identity of the nation is freed to assume a different form—if the orthodox are willing to walk out of their orthodox cages. The reasons for renouncing religion in order to break out of the voluntary ghetto have disappeared also.

At the same time, the Jewish nation is united on Jewish soil in circumstances which make it almost perverse to deny that the people have passed through a religious experience. There has been a terrible wave of persecution; there has been the miracle of the birth of the State; there has been the deliverance from the invading Arabs; there has been the Ingathering; and now there is the struggle demanding a unity which accepts the significance of all these things.

The Jews have come to one of the greatest turning points in their long history. The most important event for them of the past 2,000 years has taken place in the life of this generation.

This situation was brought about by the Zionist Movement which propagated the spirit of the Kibbutzim and the colonization of Palestine, and which still is the force directing the spirit of World Jewry towards the problems of Israel.

Zionism gave a new impulse both to the religious and to the agnostic Jews. But now, with the Ingathering, the position of orthodox and agnostic alike has been altered. It is no longer necessary for the Jewish religion to be refrigerated for fear that if it become unfrozen, the Jewish soul will be melted away into the dispersal. On the other hand, the agnostic has shared in a great religious experience; a fact which is revealed in his attempts to rewrite the services of religious festivities to describe his experience in his own agnostic terms.

The Jewish religion has, it seems to me, come to a place in its history where it has to incorporate a new stage of history within its observances. The Jews have to find their unity within this piety: within what Dr. Lehmann called their *Ehrfurcht*.

These thoughts have taken me further afield than I had intended. So I return once more to the children.

That the children of Youth Aliyah should be educated to think of themselves as Israelis and to put aside their differences of origin and colour, is most hopeful. Yet as things are to-day in Israel, there is one great flaw in this idea. While being taught to forget the colour of their skins, the children are enlisted by the education of Israel to enter into the views of ideologies. It has been easier for the educators to tell them to merge all their separate tongues in the one language of Hebrew, than to give them a background of faith common to all. They are educated to hold different political views and to practise different ways of living. So that in taking away physical barriers, the Israelis set up spiritual and ideological ones. Yet just to set up a "liberal" education in place of a sectarian one does not seem to answer the problems of Israel. What is needed is education to a faith in the new Israel as practised by the new Jews, which is the common ground on which all stand, however they diverge afterwards, and however varied are their lives as individuals. So the children bring us back to the adults, and the adults to the children.

Date Due

OCT 2 0 1961		
NOV 1 0 1961		
DEC 1 5 1961		
JAN 5 1962		
JAN 2 6 1962		
FEB 2 1962		
DEC 7 1962		
JAN 2 5 1963		
DEC 1 1 '64		
NOV 4 '66		
DEC '66		
OCT 27		
DEC 2 0 '67		
MAY 3 68		